GO!

with

Basic Computer Concepts

Getting Started

Shelley Gaskin and Diane M. Coyle

PEARSON

Prentice
Hall

Upper Saddle River, New Jersey

This book is dedicated to my students, who inspire me every day, and to my husband, Fred Gaskin.
—Shelley Gaskin

With heartfelt gratitude and love to my parents for their encouragement and support, to my children for humoring me, and to my friends for always believing in me—even when I wasn't too sure myself! You're the best!
—Diane M. Coyle

Library of Congress Cataloging-in-Publication Data

Gaskin, Shelley.
 Go! Getting started with basic computer concepts/Shelley Gaskin and Diane Coyle.
  p. cm.
Includes index.
ISBN 0-13-232793-7
1. Microcomputers. I. Coyle, Diane, 1958- II. Title
QA76.5.G3273 2007
004.16—dc22

2007009638

Vice President and Publisher: Natalie E. Anderson
Associate VP/Executive Acquisitions Editor, Print: Stephanie Wall
Executive Acquisitions Editor, Media: Richard Keaveny
Product Development Manager: Eileen Bien Calabro Sr.
Editorial Project Manager: Laura Burgess
Development Editor: Ginny Munroe
Editorial Assistants: Becky Knauer, Lora Cimiluca
Content Development Manager: Cathi Profitko
Production Media Project Manager: Lorena Cerisano
Senior Media Project Manager: Steve Gagliostro
Director of Marketing: Margaret Waples
Senior Marketing Manager: Jason Sakos
Sales Associate: Rebecca Scott
Managing Editor: Lynda J. Castillo

Production Project Manager/Buyer: Wanda Rockwell
Production Editor: GGS Book Services
Photo Researcher: GGS Book Services
Manufacturing Buyer: Natacha Moore
Production/Editorial Assistant: Andrea Shearer, Sandra K. Bernales
Design Director: Maria Lange
Art Director/Interior Design: Blair Brown
Cover Photo: Courtesy of Getty Images, Inc./Marvin Mattelson
Composition: GGS Book Services
Project Management: Kevin Bradley, GGS Book Services
Cover Printer: Phoenix Color
Printer/Binder: Courier

Microsoft, Windows, Word, PowerPoint, Outlook, FrontPage, Visual Basic, MSN, The Microsoft Network, and/or other Microsoft products referenced herein are either trademarks or registered trademarks of Microsoft Corporation in the U.S.A. and other countries. Screen shots and icons reprinted with permission from the Microsoft Corporation. This book is not sponsored or endorsed by or affiliated with Microsoft Corporation.

Credits and acknowledgments borrowed from other sources and reproduced, with permission, in this textbook are on the appropriate page within the text.

10
ISBN 10: 0-13-232793-7
ISBN 13: 978-0-13-232793-0

Table of Contents

Letter from the Editor

Dear Instructors and Students,

The primary goal of the *GO!* Series is two-fold. The first goal is to help instructors teach the course they want in less time. The second goal is to provide students with the skills to solve business problems using the computer as a tool, for both themselves and the organization for which they might be employed.

The *GO!* Series was originally created by Series Editor Shelley Gaskin and published with the release of Microsoft Office 2003. Her ideas came from years of using textbooks that didn't meet all the needs of today's diverse classroom and that were too confusing for students. Shelley continues to enhance the series by ensuring we stay true to our vision of developing quality instruction and useful classroom tools.

But we also need your input and ideas.

Over time, the *GO!* Series has evolved based on direct feedback from instructors and students using the series. *We are the publisher that listens.* To publish a textbook that works for you, it's critical that we continue to listen to this feedback. It's important to me to talk with you and hear your stories about using *GO!* Your voice can make a difference.

My hope is that this letter will inspire you to write me an e-mail and share your thoughts on using the *GO!* Series.

Stephanie Wall
Executive Editor, *GO!* Series
stephanie_wall@prenhall.com

GO! System Contributors

We thank the following people for their hard work and support in making the *GO!* System all that it is!

Additional Author Support

Coyle, Diane	Montgomery County Community College
Fry, Susan	Boise State
Townsend, Kris	Spokane Falls Community College
Stroup, Tracey	Amgen Corporation

Instructor Resource Authors

Amer, Beverly	Northern Arizona University	Paterson, Jim	Paradise Valley Community College
Boito, Nancy	Harrisburg Area Community College	Prince, Lisa	Missouri State
Coyle, Diane	Montgomery County Community College	Rodgers, Gwen	Southern Nazarene University
Dawson, Tamara	Southern Nazarene University	Ruymann, Amy	Burlington Community College
Driskel, Loretta	Niagara County Community College	Ryan, Bob	Montgomery County Community College
Elliott, Melissa	Odessa College		
Fry, Susan	Boise State	Smith, Diane	Henry Ford College
Geoghan, Debra	Bucks County Community College	Spangler, Candice	Columbus State Community College
Hearn, Barbara	Community College of Philadelphia	Thompson, Joyce	Lehigh Carbon Community College
Jones, Stephanie	South Plains College	Tiffany, Janine	Reading Area Community College
Madsen, Donna	Kirkwood Community College	Watt, Adrienne	Douglas College
Meck, Kari	Harrisburg Area Community College	Weaver, Paul	Bossier Parish Community College
Miller, Cindy	Ivy Tech	Weber, Sandy	Gateway Technical College
Nowakowski, Tony	Buffalo State	Wood, Dawn	
Pace, Phyllis	Queensborough Community College	Weissman, Jonathan	Finger Lakes Community College

Super Reviewers

Brotherton, Cathy	Riverside Community College	Maurer, Trina	Odessa College
Cates, Wally	Central New Mexico Community College	Meck, Kari	Harrisburg Area Community College
		Miller, Cindy	Ivy Tech Community College
Cone, Bill	Northern Arizona University	Nielson, Phil	Salt Lake Community College
Coverdale, John	Riverside Community College	Rodgers, Gwen	Southern Nazarene University
Foster, Nancy	Baker College	Smolenski, Robert	Delaware Community College
Helfand, Terri	Chaffey College	Spangler, Candice	Columbus State Community College
Hibbert, Marilyn	Salt Lake Community College	Thompson, Joyce	Lehigh Carbon Community College
Holliday, Mardi	Community College of Philadelphia	Weber, Sandy	Gateway Technical College
Jerry, Gina	Santa Monica College	Wells, Lorna	Salt Lake Community College
Martin, Carol	Harrisburg Area Community College	Zaboski, Maureen	University of Scranton

Technical Editors

Janice Snyder
Joyce Nielsen
Colette Eisele
Janet Pickard
Mara Zebest
Lindsey Allen
William Daley

Student Reviewers

Allen, John	Asheville-Buncombe Tech Community College	Erickson, Mike	Ball State University
		Gadomski, Amanda	Northern Michigan University
Alexander, Steven	St. Johns River Community College	Gyselinck, Craig	Central Washington University
Alexander, Melissa	Tulsa Community College	Harrison, Margo	Central Washington University
Bolz, Stephanie	Northern Michigan University	Heacox, Kate	Central Washington University
Berner, Ashley	Central Washington University	Hill, Cheretta	Northwestern State University
Boomer, Michelle	Northern Michigan University	Innis, Tim	Tulsa Community College
Busse, Brennan	Northern Michigan University	Jarboe, Aaron	Central Washington University
Butkey, Maura	Central Washington University	Klein, Colleen	Northern Michigan University
Christensen, Kaylie	Northern Michigan University	Moeller, Jeffrey	Northern Michigan University
Connally, Brianna	Central Washington University	Nicholson, Regina	Athens Tech College
Davis, Brandon	Northern Michigan University	Niehaus, Kristina	Northern Michigan University
Davis, Christen	Central Washington University	Nisa, Zaibun	Santa Rosa Community College
Den Boer, Lance	Central Washington University	Nunez, Nohelia	Santa Rosa Community College
Dix, Jessica	Central Washington University	Oak, Samantha	Central Washington University
Moeller, Jeffrey	Northern Michigan University	Oertii, Monica	Central Washington University
Downs, Elizabeth	Central Washington University	Palenshus, Juliet	Central Washington University

Pohl, Amanda	Northern Michigan University	Shanahan, Megan	Northern Michigan University
Presnell, Randy	Central Washington University	Teska, Erika	Hawaii Pacific University
Ritner, April	Northern Michigan University	Traub, Amy	Northern Michigan University
Rodriguez, Flavia	Northwestern State University	Underwood, Katie	Central Washington University
Roberts, Corey	Tulsa Community College	Walters, Kim	Central Washington University
Rossi, Jessica Ann	Central Washington University	Wilson, Kelsie	Central Washington University
Shafapay, Natasha	Central Washington University	Wilson, Amanda	Green River Community College

Series Reviewers

Abraham, Reni	Houston Community College	Crawford, Thomasina	Miami-Dade College, Kendall Campus
Agatston, Ann	Agatston Consulting Technical College	Credico, Grace	Lethbridge Community College
		Crenshaw, Richard	Miami Dade Community College, North
Alexander, Melody	Ball Sate University		
Alejandro, Manuel	Southwest Texas Junior College	Crespo, Beverly	Mt. San Antonio College
Ali, Farha	Lander University	Crossley, Connie	Cincinnati State Technical Community College
Amici, Penny	Harrisburg Area Community College		
Anderson, Patty A.	Lake City Community College	Curik, Mary	Central New Mexico Community College
Andrews, Wilma	Virginia Commonwealth College, Nebraska University		
		De Arazoza, Ralph	Miami Dade Community College
Anik, Mazhar	Tiffin University	Danno, John	DeVry University/Keller Graduate School
Armstrong, Gary	Shippensburg University		
Atkins, Bonnie	Delaware Technical Community College	Davis, Phillip	Del Mar College
		DeHerrera, Laurie	Pikes Peak Community College
Bachand, LaDonna	Santa Rosa Community College	Delk, Dr. K. Kay	Seminole Community College
Bagui, Sikha	University of West Florida	Doroshow, Mike	Eastfield College
Beecroft, Anita	Kwantlen University College	Douglas, Gretchen	SUNYCortland
Bell, Paula	Lock Haven College	Dove, Carol	Community College of Allegheny
Belton, Linda	Springfield Tech. Community College	Driskel, Loretta	Niagara Community College
		Duckwiler, Carol	Wabaunsee Community College
Bennett, Judith	Sam Houston State University	Duncan, Mimi	University of Missouri-St. Louis
Bhatia, Sai	Riverside Community College	Duthie, Judy	Green River Community College
Bishop, Frances	DeVry Institute—Alpharetta (ATL)	Duvall, Annette	Central New Mexico Community College
Blaszkiewicz, Holly	Ivy Tech Community College/Region 1		
Branigan, Dave	DeVry University	Ecklund, Paula	Duke University
Bray, Patricia	Allegany College of Maryland	Eng, Bernice	Brookdale Community College
Brotherton, Cathy	Riverside Community College	Evans, Billie	Vance-Granville Community College
Buehler, Lesley	Ohlone College	Feuerbach, Lisa	Ivy Tech East Chicago
Buell, C	Central Oregon Community College	Fisher, Fred	Florida State University
Byars, Pat	Brookhaven College	Foster, Penny L.	Anne Arundel Community College
Byrd, Lynn	Delta State University, Cleveland, Mississippi	Foszcz, Russ	McHenry County College
		Fry, Susan	Boise State University
Cacace, Richard N.	Pensacola Junior College	Fustos, Janos	Metro State
Cadenhead, Charles	Brookhaven College	Gallup, Jeanette	Blinn College
Calhoun, Ric	Gordon College	Gelb, Janet	Grossmont College
Cameron, Eric	Passaic Community College	Gentry, Barb	Parkland College
Carriker, Sandra	North Shore Community College	Gerace, Karin	St. Angela Merici School
Cannamore, Madie	Kennedy King	Gerace, Tom	Tulane University
Carreon, Cleda	Indiana University—Purdue University, Indianapolis	Ghajar, Homa	Oklahoma State University
		Gifford, Steve	Northwest Iowa Community College
Chaffin, Catherine	Shawnee State University	Glazer, Ellen	Broward Community College
Chauvin, Marg	Palm Beach Community College, Boca Raton	Gordon, Robert	Hofstra University
		Gramlich, Steven	Pasco-Hernando Community College
Challa, Chandrashekar	Virginia State University	Graviett, Nancy M.	St. Charles Community College, St. Peters, Missouri
Chamlou, Afsaneh	NOVA Alexandria		
Chapman, Pam	Wabaunsee Community College	Greene, Rich	Community College of Allegheny County
Christensen, Dan	Iowa Western Community College		
Clay, Betty	Southeastern Oklahoma State University	Gregoryk, Kerry	Virginia Commonwealth State
		Griggs, Debra	Bellevue Community College
Collins, Linda D.	Mesa Community College	Grimm, Carol	Palm Beach Community College
Conroy-Link, Janet	Holy Family College	Hahn, Norm	Thomas Nelson Community College
Cosgrove, Janet	Northwestern CT Community	Hammerschlag, Dr. Bill	Brookhaven College
Courtney, Kevin	Hillsborough Community College	Hansen, Michelle	Davenport University
Cox, Rollie	Madison Area Technical College	Hayden, Nancy	Indiana University—Purdue University, Indianapolis
Crawford, Hiram	Olive Harvey College		

Hayes, Theresa	Broward Community College
Helfand, Terri	Chaffey College
Helms, Liz	Columbus State Community College
Hernandez, Leticia	TCI College of Technology
Hibbert, Marilyn	Salt Lake Community College
Hoffman, Joan	Milwaukee Area Technical College
Hogan, Pat	Cape Fear Community College
Holland, Susan	Southeast Community College
Hopson, Bonnie	Athens Technical College
Horvath, Carrie	Albertus Magnus College
Horwitz, Steve	Community College of Philadelphia
Hotta, Barbara	Leeward Community College
Howard, Bunny	St. Johns River Community
Howard, Chris	DeVry University
Huckabay, Jamie	Austin Community College
Hudgins, Susan	East Central University
Hulett, Michelle J.	Missouri State University
Hunt, Darla A.	Morehead State University, Morehead, Kentucky
Hunt, Laura	Tulsa Community College
Jacob, Sherry	Jefferson Community College
Jacobs, Duane	Salt Lake Community College
Jauken, Barb	Southeastern Community
Johnson, Kathy	Wright College
Johnson, Mary	Kingwood College
Johnson, Mary	Mt. San Antonio College
Jones, Stacey	Benedict College
Jones, Warren	University of Alabama, Birmingham
Jordan, Cheryl	San Juan College
Kapoor, Bhushan	California State University, Fullerton
Kasai, Susumu	Salt Lake Community College
Kates, Hazel	Miami Dade Community College, Kendall
Keen, Debby	University of Kentucky
Keeter, Sandy	Seminole Community College
Kern-Blystone, Dorothy Jean	Bowling Green State
Keskin, Ilknur	The University of South Dakota
Kirk, Colleen	Mercy College
Kleckner, Michelle	Elon University
Kliston, Linda	Broward Community College, North Campus
Kochis, Dennis	Suffolk County Community College
Kramer, Ed	Northern Virginia Community College
Laird, Jeff	Northeast State Community College
Lamoureaux, Jackie	Central New Mexico Community College
Lange, David	Grand Valley State
LaPointe, Deb	Central New Mexico Community College
Larson, Donna	Louisville Technical Institute
Laspina, Kathy	Vance-Granville Community College
Le Grand, Dr. Kate	Broward Community College
Lenhart, Sheryl	Terra Community College
Letavec, Chris	University of Cincinnati
Liefert, Jane	Everett Community College
Lindaman, Linda	Black Hawk Community College
Lindberg, Martha	Minnesota State University
Lightner, Renee	Broward Community College
Lindberg, Martha	Minnesota State University
Linge, Richard	Arizona Western College
Logan, Mary G.	Delgado Community College
Loizeaux, Barbara	Westchester Community College
Lopez, Don	Clovis-State Center Community College District

Lord, Alexandria	Asheville Buncombe Tech
Lowe, Rita	Harold Washington College
Low, Willy Hui	Joliet Junior College
Lucas, Vickie	Broward Community College
Lynam, Linda	Central Missouri State University
Lyon, Lynne	Durham College
Lyon, Pat Rajski	Tomball College
MacKinnon, Ruth	Georgia Southern University
Macon, Lisa	Valencia Community College, West Campus
Machuca, Wayne	College of the Sequoias
Madison, Dana	Clarion University
Maguire, Trish	Eastern New Mexico University
Malkan, Rajiv	Montgomery College
Manning, David	Northern Kentucky University
Marcus, Jacquie	Niagara Community College
Marghitu, Daniela	Auburn University
Marks, Suzanne	Bellevue Community College
Marquez, Juanita	El Centro College
Marquez, Juan	Mesa Community College
Martyn, Margie	Baldwin-Wallace College
Marucco, Toni	Lincoln Land Community College
Mason, Lynn	Lubbock Christian University
Matutis, Audrone	Houston Community College
Matkin, Marie	University of Lethbridge
McCain, Evelynn	Boise State University
McCannon, Melinda	Gordon College
McCarthy, Marguerite	Northwestern Business College
McCaskill, Matt L.	Brevard Community College
McClellan, Carolyn	Tidewater Community College
McClure, Darlean	College of Sequoias
McCrory, Sue A.	Missouri State University
McCue, Stacy	Harrisburg Area Community College
McEntire-Orbach, Teresa	Middlesex County College
McLeod, Todd	Fresno City College
McManus, Illyana	Grossmont College
McPherson, Dori	Schoolcraft College
Meiklejohn, Nancy	Pikes Peak Community College
Menking, Rick	Hardin-Simmons University
Meredith, Mary	University of Louisiana at Lafayette
Mermelstein, Lisa	Baruch College
Metos, Linda	Salt Lake Community College
Meurer, Daniel	University of Cincinnati
Meyer, Marian	Central New Mexico Community College
Miller, Cindy	Ivy Tech Community College, Lafayette, Indiana
Mitchell, Susan	Davenport University
Mohle, Dennis	Fresno Community College
Monk, Ellen	University of Delaware
Moore, Rodney	Holland College
Morris, Mike	Southeastern Oklahoma State University
Morris, Nancy	Hudson Valley Community College
Moseler, Dan	Harrisburg Area Community College
Nabors, Brent	Reedley College, Clovis Center
Nadas, Erika	Wright College
Nadelman, Cindi	New England College
Nademlynsky, Lisa	Johnson & Wales University
Ncube, Cathy	University of West Florida
Nagengast, Joseph	Florida Career College
Newsome, Eloise	Northern Virginia Community College Woodbridge
Nicholls, Doreen	Mohawk Valley Community College
Nunan, Karen	Northeast State Technical Community College

Odegard, Teri	Edmonds Community College	Sterling, Janet	Houston Community College
Ogle, Gregory	North Community College	Stoughton, Catherine	Laramie County Community College
Orr, Dr. Claudia	Northern Michigan University South	Sullivan, Angela	Joliet Junior College
Otieno, Derek	DeVry University	Szurek, Joseph	University of Pittsburgh at Greensburg
Otton, Diana Hill	Chesapeake College	Tarver, Mary Beth	Northwestern State University
Oxendale, Lucia	West Virginia Institute of Technology	Taylor, Michael	Seattle Central Community College
Paiano, Frank	Southwestern College	Thangiah, Sam	Slippery Rock University
Patrick, Tanya	Clackamas Community College	Thompson-Sellers, Ingrid	Georgia Perimeter College
Peairs, Deb	Clark State Community College	Tomasi, Erik	Baruch College
Prince, Lisa	Missouri State University-Springfield Campus	Toreson, Karen	Shoreline Community College
Proietti, Kathleen	Northern Essex Community College	Trifiletti, John J.	Florida Community College at Jacksonville
Pusins, Delores	HCCC	Trivedi, Charulata	Quinsigamond Community College, Woodbridge
Raghuraman, Ram	Joliet Junior College	Tucker, William	Austin Community College
Reasoner, Ted Allen	Indiana University—Purdue	Turgeon, Cheryl	Asnuntuck Community College
Reeves, Karen	High Point University	Turpen, Linda	Central New Mexico Community College
Remillard, Debbie	New Hampshire Technical Institute		
Rhue, Shelly	DeVry University	Upshaw, Susan	Del Mar College
Richards, Karen	Maplewoods Community College	Unruh, Angela	Central Washington University
Richardson, Mary	Albany Technical College	Vanderhoof, Dr. Glenna	Missouri State University-Springfield Campus
Rodgers, Gwen	Southern Nazarene University	Vargas, Tony	El Paso Community College
Roselli, Diane	Harrisburg Area Community College	Vicars, Mitzi	Hampton University
Ross, Dianne	University of Louisiana in Lafayette	Villarreal, Kathleen	Fresno
Rousseau, Mary	Broward Community College, South	Vitrano, Mary Ellen	Palm Beach Community College
Samson, Dolly	Hawaii Pacific University	Volker, Bonita	Tidewater Community College
Sams, Todd	University of Cincinnati	Wahila, Lori (Mindy)	Tompkins Cortland Community College
Sandoval, Everett	Reedley College		
Sardone, Nancy	Seton Hall University	Waswick, Kim	Southeast Community College, Nebraska
Scafide, Jean	Mississippi Gulf Coast Community College	Wavle, Sharon	Tompkins Cortland Community College
Scheeren, Judy	Westmoreland County Community College	Webb, Nancy	City College of San Francisco
Schneider, Sol	Sam Houston State University	Wells, Barbara E.	Central Carolina Technical College
Scroggins, Michael	Southwest Missouri State University	Wells, Lorna	Salt Lake Community College
Sever, Suzanne	Northwest Arkansas Community College	Welsh, Jean	Lansing Community College Nebraska
Sheridan, Rick	California State University-Chico	White, Bruce	Quinnipiac University
Silvers, Pamela	Asheville Buncombe Tech	Willer, Ann	Solano Community College
Singer, Steven A.	University of Hawai'i, Kapi'olani Community College	Williams, Mark	Lane Community College
Sinha, Atin	Albany State University	Wilson, Kit	Red River College
Skolnick, Martin	Florida Atlantic University	Wilson, Roger	Fairmont State University
Smith, T. Michael	Austin Community College	Wimberly, Leanne	International Academy of Design and Technology
Smith, Tammy	Tompkins Cortland Community Collge	Worthington, Paula	Northern Virginia Community College
Smolenski, Bob	Delaware County Community College	Yauney, Annette	Herkimer County Community College
Spangler, Candice	Columbus State	Yip, Thomas	Passaic Community College
Stedham, Vicki	St. Petersburg College, Clearwater	Zavala, Ben	Webster Tech
Stefanelli, Greg	Carroll Community College	Zlotow, Mary Ann	College of DuPage
Steiner, Ester	New Mexico State University	Zudeck, Steve	Broward Community College, North
Stenlund, Neal	Northern Virginia Community College, Alexandria		
St. John, Steve	Tulsa Community College		

About the Author

Shelley Gaskin, Series Editor, is a professor of business and computer technology at Pasadena City College in Pasadena, California. She holds a master's degree in business education from Northern Illinois University and a doctorate in adult and community education from Ball State University. Dr. Gaskin has 15 years of experience in the computer industry with several Fortune 500 companies and has developed and written training materials for custom systems applications in both the public and private sector. She is also the author of books on Microsoft Outlook and word processing.

Diane M. Coyle is an adjunct instructor and full-time administrator at Montgomery County Community College in Blue Bell, Pennsylvania, where she has been teaching computer literacy, office applications, and Web design classes for more than six years. Her work in the fields of marketing and project management helps her to present a balanced and practical focus to the information she shares with her students.

Visual Walk-Through of the *GO!* System

The *GO!* System is designed for ease of implementation on the instructor side and ease of understanding on the student. It has been completely developed based on professor and student feedback.

The *GO!* System is divided into three categories that reflect how you might organize your course—**Prepare**, **Teach**, and **Assess**.

Prepare

NEW

Transition Guide

New to *GO!*—We've made it quick and easy to plan the format and activities for your class.

Syllabus Template

Includes course calendar planner for 8-, 12-, and 16-week formats.

GO!

Because the GO! System was designed and written by instructors like yourself, it includes the tools that allow you to Prepare, Teach, and Assess in your course. We have organized the GO! System into these three categories that match how you work through your course and thus, it's even easier for you to implement.

To help you get started, here is an outline of the first activities you may want to do in order to conduct your course.

There are several other tools not listed here that are available in the GO! System so please refer to your GO! Guide for a complete listing of all the tools.

Prepare
1. Prepare the course syllabus
2. Plan the course assignments
3. Organize the student resources

Teach
4. Conduct demonstrations and lectures

Assess
5. Assign and grade assignments, quizzes, tests, and assessments

PREPARE

1. Prepare the course syllabus

A syllabus template is provided on the IRCD in the **go07_syllabus_template** folder of the main directory. It includes a course calendar planner for 8-week, 12-week, and 16-week formats. Depending on your term (summer or regular semester) you can modify one of these according to your course plan, and then add information pertinent to your course and institution.

2. Plan course assignments

For each chapter, an Assignment Sheet listing every in-chapter and end-of-chapter project is located on the IRCD within the **go01_gooffice2007intro_instructor_resources_by_chapter** folder. From there, navigate to the specific chapter folder. These sheets are Word tables, so you can delete rows for the projects that you choose not to assign or add rows for your own assignments—if any. There is a column to add the number of points you want to assign to each project depending on your grading scheme. At the top of the sheet, you can fill in the course information.

Transitioning to GO! Office 2007 — Page 1 of 1

GO! with Microsoft Office 2007 Introductory
SAMPLE SYLLABUS (16 weeks)

I. COURSE INFORMATION

Course No.:	Semester:
Course Title:	Credits:
Course Hours:	
Instructor:	Office:
Office Hours:	
Email:	Phone:

II. TEXT AND MATERIALS

Before starting the course, you will need the following:

- GO! with Microsoft Office 2007 Introductory by Shelley Gaskin, Robert L. Ferrett, Alicia Vargas, Suzanne Marks ©2007, published by Pearson Prentice Hall. ISBN 0-13-167990-6
- Storage device for saving files (any of the following: multiple diskettes, CD-RW, flash drive, etc.)

III. WHAT YOU WILL LEARN IN THIS COURSE

This is a hands-on course where you will learn to use a computer to practice the most commonly used Microsoft programs including the Windows operating system, Internet Explorer for navigating the Internet, Outlook for managing your personal information and the four most popular programs within the Microsoft Office Suite (Word, Excel, PowerPoint and Access). You will also practice the basics of using a computer, mouse and keyboard. You will learn to be an intermediate level user of the Microsoft Office Suite.

Within the Microsoft Office Suite, you will use Word, Excel, PowerPoint, and Access. Microsoft Word is a word processing program with which you can create common business and personal documents. Microsoft Excel is a spreadsheet program that organizes and calculates accounting-type information. Microsoft PowerPoint is a presentation graphics program with which you can develop slides to accompany an oral presentation. Finally, Microsoft Access is a database program that organizes large amounts of information in a useful manner.

Assignment Sheet

One per chapter. Lists all possible assignments; add to and delete from this simple Word table according to your course plan.

File Guide to the *GO!* Supplements

Tabular listing of all supplements and their file names.

NEW

Assignment Planning Guide

Description of *GO!* assignments with recommendations based on class size, delivery mode, and student needs. Includes examples from fellow instructors.

GO! with Microsoft Office 2007 Introductory
Assignment Planning Guide

Planning the Course Assignments

For each chapter in GO!, an Assignment Sheet listing every in-chapter and end-of-chapter project is located on the IRCD. These sheets are Word tables, so you can delete rows for the projects that you will not assign, and then add rows for any of your own assignments that you may have developed. There is a column to add the number of points you want to assign to each project—depending on your grading scheme. At the top of the sheet, you can fill in your course information.

Additionally, for each chapter, student Assignment Tags are provided for every project (including Problem Solving projects)—also located on the IRCD. These are small scoring checklists on which you can check off errors made by the student, and with which the student can verify that all project elements are complete. For campus classes, the student can attach the tags to his or her paper submissions. For online classes, many GO! instructors have the student include these with the electronic submission.

Deciding What to Assign

Front Portion of the Chapter—Instructional Projects: The projects in the front portion of the chapter, which are listed on the first page of each chapter, are the instructional projects. Most instructors assign all of these projects, because this is where the student receives the instruction and engages in the active learning.

End-of-Chapter—Practice and Critical Thinking Projects: In the back portion of the chapter (the gray pages), you can assign on a prescriptive basis; that is, for students who were challenged by the instructional projects, you might assign one or more projects from the two *Skills Reviews*, which provide maximum prompting and a thorough review of the entire chapter. For students who have previous software knowledge and who completed the instructional projects easily, you might assign only the *Mastery Projects*.

You can also assign prescriptively by Objective, because each end-of-chapter project indicates the Objectives covered. So you might assign, on a student-by-student basis, only the projects that cover the Objectives with which the student seemed to have difficulty in the instructional projects.

The five Problem Solving projects and the You and GO! project are the authentic assessments that pull together the student's learning. Here the student is presented with a "messy real-life situation" and then uses his or her knowledge and skill to solve a problem, produce a product, give a presentation, or demonstrate a procedure. You might assign one or more of the Problem

GO! Assignment Planning Guide   Page 1 of 1

Student Data Files

Online Study Guide for Students
Interactive objective-style questions based on chapter content.

PowerPoint Slides

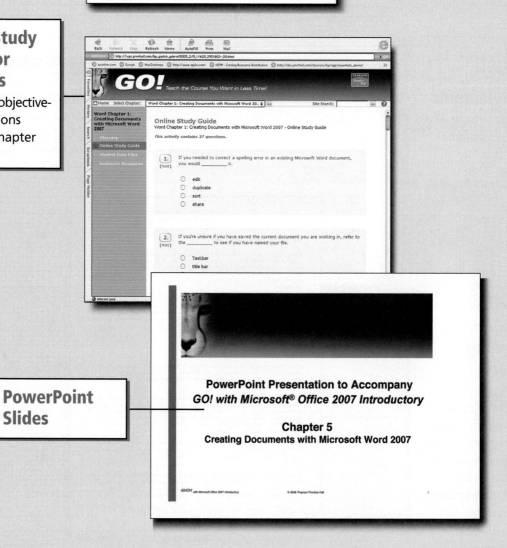

Student Textbook

Learning Objectives and Student Outcomes

Objectives are clustered around projects that result in student outcomes. They help students learn how to solve problems, not just learn software features.

Project-Based Instruction

Students do not practice features of the application; they create real projects that they will need in the real world. Projects are color coded for easy reference and are named to reflect skills the students will be practicing.

A and B Projects

Each chapter contains two instructional projects—A and B.

Word 2007

5 chapterfive
Creating Documents with Microsoft Word 2007

OBJECTIVES
At the end of this chapter you will be able to:

OUTCOMES
Mastering these objectives will enable you to:

1. Create and Save a New Document
2. Edit Text
3. Select, Delete, and Format Text
4. Print a Document

PROJECT 5A
Create, Edit, Save, and Print a Document

5. Navigate the Word Window
6. Add a Graphic to a Document
7. Use the Spelling and Grammar Checker
8. Preview and Print Documents, Close a Document, and Close Word
9. Use the Microsoft Help System

PROJECT 5B
Navigate the Word Window and Check Your Work

NEW

Word 237

Music School Records

Music School Records was created to launch young musical artists with undiscovered talent in jazz, classical, and contemporary music. The creative management team searches internationally for talented young people, and has a reputation for mentoring and developing the skills of its artists. The company's music is tailored to an audience that is young, knowledgeable about music, and demands the highest quality recordings. Music School Records releases are available in CD format as well as digital downloads.

Getting Started with Microsoft Office Word 2007

A word processor is the most common program found on personal computers and one that almost everyone has a reason to use. When you learn word processing you are also learning skills and techniques that you need to work efficiently on a personal computer. You can use Microsoft Word to perform basic word processing tasks such as writing a memo, a report, or a letter. You can also use Word to complete complex word processing tasks, such as those that include sophisticated tables, embedded graphics, and links to other documents and the Internet. Word is a program that you can learn gradually, and then add more advanced skills one at a time.

Each chapter opens with a story that sets the stage for the projects the student will create; the instruction does not force the student to pretend to be someone or make up a scenario.

Each chapter has an introductory paragraph that briefs students on what is important.

Visual Summary

Shows students upfront what their projects will look like when they are done.

Project Summary

Stated clearly and quickly in one paragraph.

NEW

File Guide

Clearly shows students which files are needed for the project and the names they will use to save their documents.

Objective

The skills the student will learn are clearly stated at the beginning of each project and color coded to match projects listed on the chapter opener page.

Teachable Moment

Expository text is woven into the steps—at the moment students need to know it—not chunked together in a block of text that will go unread.

NEW

Screen Shots

Larger screen shots.

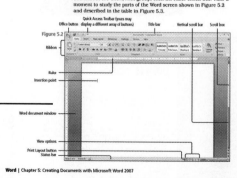

Steps

Color coded to the current project, easy to read, and not too many to confuse the student or too few to be meaningless.

Sequential Pagination

No more confusing letters and abbreviations.

End-of-Project Icon

All projects in the *GO! Series* have clearly identifiable end points, useful in self-paced or on-line environments.

Microsoft Procedural Syntax

All steps are written in Microsoft Procedural Syntax to put the student in the right place at the right time.

---

5 Press Enter two more times.

In a business letter, insert two blank lines between the date and the inside address, which is the same as the address you would use on an envelope.

6 Type **Mr. William Hawken** and then press Enter.

The wavy red line under the proper name *Hawken* indicates that the word has been flagged as misspelled because it is a word not contained in the Word dictionary.

7 On two lines, type the following address, but do not press Enter at the end of the second line:

123 Eighth Street
Harrisville, MI 48740

> **Note — Typing the Address**
>
> Include a comma after the city name in an inside address. However, for mailing addresses on envelopes, eliminate the comma after the city name.

8 On the **Home tab**, in the **Styles group**, click the **Normal** button.

The Normal style is applied to the text in the rest of the document. Recall that the Normal style adds extra space between paragraphs; it also adds slightly more space between lines in a paragraph.

9 Press Enter. Type **Dear William:** and then press Enter.

This salutation is the line that greets the person receiving the letter.

10 Type **Subject: Your Application to Music School Records** and press Enter. Notice the light dots between words, which indicate spaces and display when formatting marks are displayed. Also, notice the extra space after each paragraph, and then compare your screen with Figure 5.6.

The subject line is optional, but you should include a subject line in most letters to identify the topic. Depending on your Word settings, a wavy green line may display in the subject line, indicating a potential grammar error.

244 Word | Chapter 5: Creating Documents with Microsoft Word 2007

> **Note — Space Between Lines in Your Printed Document**
>
> The Cambria font, and many others, uses a slightly larger space between the lines than more traditional fonts like Times New Roman. As you progress in your study of Word, you will use many different fonts and also adjust the spacing between lines.

3 From the **Office** menu, click **Close**, saving any changes if prompted to do so. Leave Word open for the next project.

Another Way | **To Print a Document**

To Print a document:

- From the Office menu, click Print to display the Print dialog box (to be covered later), from which you can choose a variety of different options, such as printing multiple copies, printing on a different printer, and printing some but not all pages.
- Hold down Ctrl and then press P. This is an alternative to the Office menu command, and opens the Print dialog box.
- Hold down Alt, press F, and then press P. This opens the Print dialog box.

End You have completed Project 5A

264 Word | Chapter 5: Creating Documents with Microsoft Word 2007

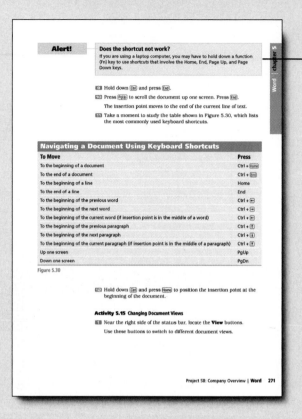

Alert box

Draws students' attention to make sure they aren't getting too far off course.

Another Way box

Shows students other ways of doing tasks.

More Knowledge box

Expands on a topic by going deeper into the material.

Note box

Points out important items to remember.

There's More You Can Do!

Try IT! exercises that teach students additional skills.

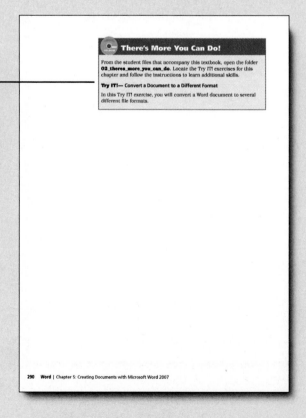

End-of-Chapter Material

Take your pick! Content-based or Outcomes-based projects to choose from. Below is a table outlining the various types of projects that fit into these two categories.

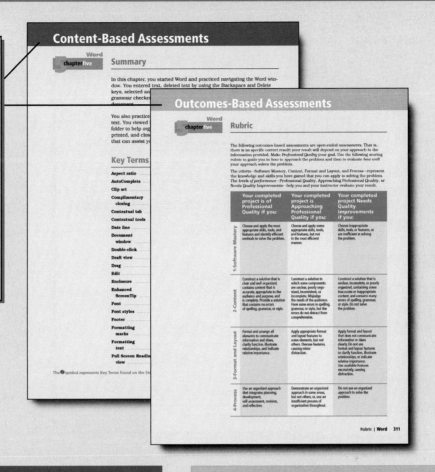

Content-Based Assessments
(Defined solutions with solution files provided for grading)

Project Letter	Name	Objectives Covered
N/A	Summary and Key Terms	
N/A	Multiple Choice	
N/A	Fill-in-the-blank	
C	Skills Review	Covers A Objectives
D	Skills Review	Covers B Objectives
E	Mastering Excel	Covers A Objectives
F	Mastering Excel	Covers B Objectives
G	Mastering Excel	Covers any combination of A and B Objectives
H	Mastering Excel	Covers any combination of A and B Objectives
I	Mastering Excel	Covers all A and B Objectives
J	Business Running Case	Covers all A and B Objectives

Outcomes-Based Assessments
(Open solutions that require a rubric for grading)

Project Letter	Name	Objectives Covered
N/A	Rubric	
K	Problem Solving	Covers as many Objectives from A and B as possible
L	Problem Solving	Covers as many Objectives from A and B as possible.
M	Problem Solving	Covers as many Objectives from A and B as possible.
N	Problem Solving	Covers as many Objectives from A and B as possible.
O	Problem Solving	Covers as many Objectives from A and B as possible.
P	You and GO!	Covers as many Objectives from A and B as possible
Q	GO! Help	Not tied to specific objectives
R	* Group Business Running Case	Covers A and B Objectives

* This project is provided only with the *GO! with Microsoft Office 2007 Introductory* book.

Objectives List

Most projects in the end-of-chapter section begin with a list of the objectives covered.

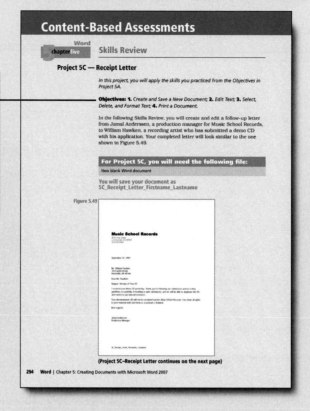

End of Each Project Clearly Marked

Clearly identified end points help separate the end-of-chapter projects.

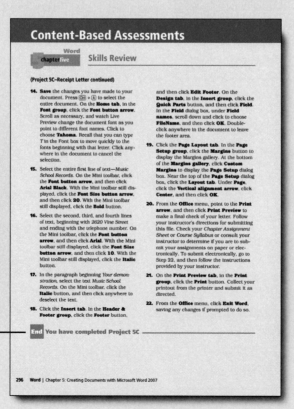

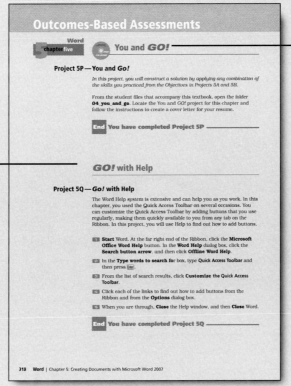

NEW

Rubric
A matrix that states the criteria and standards for grading student work. Used to grade open-ended assessments.

GO! with Help
Students practice using the Help feature of the Office application.

NEW

You and GO!
A project in which students use information from their own lives and apply the skills from the chapter to a personal task.

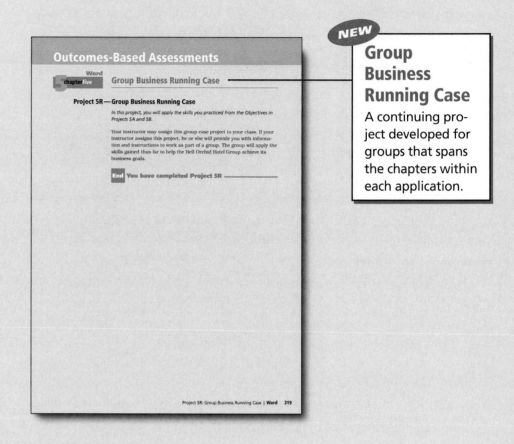

Group Business Running Case

A continuing project developed for groups that spans the chapters within each application.

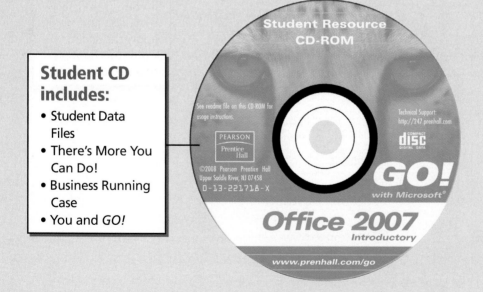

Student CD includes:

- Student Data Files
- There's More You Can Do!
- Business Running Case
- You and GO!

Companion Web site

An interactive Web site to further student leaning.

Online Study Guide

Interactive objective-style questions to help students study.

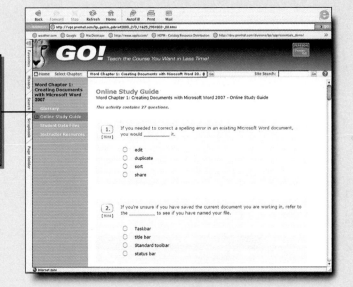

Annotated Instructor Edition

The Annotated Instructor Edition contains a full version of the student textbook that includes tips, supplement references, and pointers on teaching with the *GO!* instructional system.

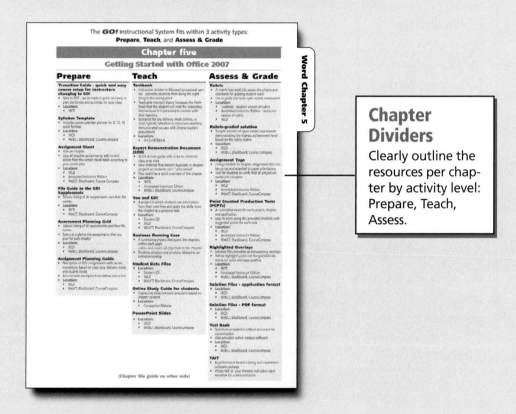

Chapter Dividers

Clearly outline the resources per chapter by activity level: Prepare, Teach, Assess.

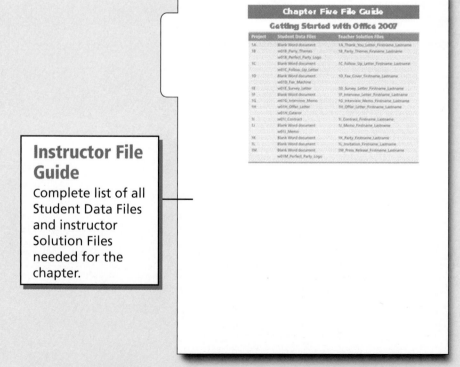

Instructor File Guide

Complete list of all Student Data Files and instructor Solution Files needed for the chapter.

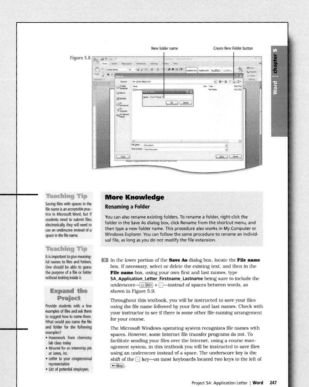

Helpful Hints, Teaching Tips, Expand the Project

References correspond to what is being taught in the student textbook.

Full-Size Textbook Pages

An instructor copy of the textbook with traditional Instructor Manual content incorporated.

End-of-Chapter Concepts Assessments

contain the answers for quick reference.

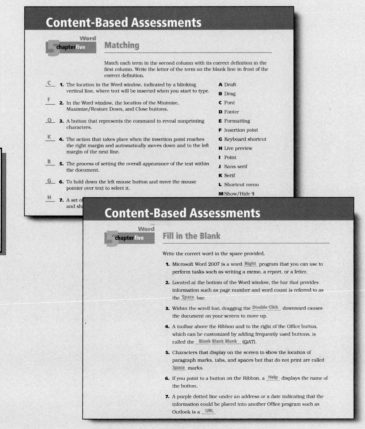

NEW

Rubric

A matrix to guide the student on how they will be assessed is reprinted in the Annotated Instructor Edition with suggested weights for each of the criteria and levels of performance. Instructors can modify the weights to suit their needs.

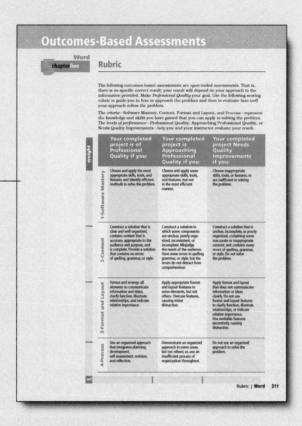

Assignment Tags

NEW

Scoring checklist for assignments. Now also available for Problem-Solving projects.

GO! with Microsoft® Office 2007

Assignment Tags for GO! with Office 2007
Word Chapter 5

Name:	Project:	5A	Name:	Project:	5B
Professor:	Course:		Professor:	Course:	
Task	**Points**	**Your Score**	**Task**	**Points**	**Your Score**
Center text vertically on page	2		Insert the file w05B_Music_School_Records	4	
Delete the word "really"	1		Insert the Music Logo	4	
Delete the words "try to"	1		Remove duplicate "and"	2	
Replace "last" with "first"	1		Change spelling and grammar errors (4)	8	
Insert the word "potential"	1		Correct/Add footer as instructed	2	
Replace "John W. Diamond" with "Lucy Burrows"	2		Circled information is incorrect or formatted incorrectly		
Change entire document to the Cambria font	2				
Change the first line of text to Arial Black 20 pt. font	2				
Bold the first line of text	2				
Change the 2nd through 4th lines to Arial 10 pt.	2				
Italicize the 2nd through 4th lines of text	2				
Correct/Add footer as instructed	2				
Circled information is incorrect or formatted incorrectly					
Total Points	**20**	**0**	**Total Points**	**20**	**0**
Name:	Project:	5C	Name:	Project:	5D
Professor:	Course:		Professor:	Course:	
Task	**Points**	**Your Score**	**Task**	**Points**	**Your Score**
Add four line letterhead	2		Insert the file w05D_Marketing	4	
Insert today's date	1		Bold the first two title lines	2	
Add address block, subject line, and greeting	2		Correct spelling of "Marketting"	2	
Add two-paragraph body of letter	2		Correct spelling of "geners"	2	
Add closing, name, and title	2		Correct all misspellings of "allready"	2	
In subject line, capitalize "receipt"	1		Correct grammar error "are" to "is"	2	
Change "standards" to "guidelines"	1		Insert the Piano image	4	
Insert "quite"	1		Correct/add footer as instructed	2	
Insert "all"	1		Circled information is incorrect or formatted incorrectly		
Change the first line of text to Arial Black 20 pt. font	2				
Bold the first line of text	1				
Change the 2nd through 4th lines to Arial 10 pt.	1				
Italicize the 2nd through 4th lines of text	1				
Correct/add footer as instructed	2				
Circled information is incorrect or formatted incorrectly					
Total Points	**20**	**0**	**Total Points**	**20**	**0**

Highlighted Overlays

Solution files provided as transparency overlays. Yellow highlights point out the gradable elements for quick and easy grading.

Music School Records

← 20 point Arial Black, bold and underline

2620 Vine Street
Los Angeles, CA 90028
323-555-0028

← 10 point Arial, italic

September 12, 2009

Mr. William Hawken
123 Eighth Street
Harrisville, MI 48740

Text vertically centered on page

Body of document changed to Cambria font, 11 point

Dear William:

Subject: Your Application to Music School Records

Thank you for submitting your application to Music School Records. Our talent scout for Northern Michigan, Catherine McDonald, is very enthusiastic about your music, and the demo CD you submitted certainly confirms her opinion. Word "really" deleted

We discuss our applications from potential clients during the first week of each month. We will have a decision for you by the second week of October.

Yours Truly, Words "try to" deleted

Lucy Burroughs

Point-Counted Production Tests (PCPTs)

A cumulative exam for each **project**, **chapter**, and **application**. Easy to score using the provided checklist with suggested points for each task.

GO! with Microsoft® Office 2007 Introductory

Point-Counted Production Test—Project for GO! with Microsoft® Office 2007 Introductory Project 5A

Instructor Name: _____
Course Information: _____

1. Start Word 2007 to begin a new blank document. Save your document as 5A_Cover_Letter_Firstname_Lastname Remember to save your file frequently as you work.

2. If necessary, display the formatting marks. With the insertion point blinking in the upper left corner of the document to the left of the default first paragraph mark, type the current date (you can use AutoComplete).

3. Press Enter three times and type the inside address:

    Music School Records
    2620 Vine Street
    Los Angeles, CA 90028

4. Press Enter three times, and type Dear Ms. Burroughs:

    Press Enter twice, and type Subject: Application to Music School Records

    Press Enter twice, and type the following text (skipping one line between paragraphs):

    I read about Music School Records in Con Brio magazine and I would like to inquire about the possibility of being represented by your company.

    I am very interested in a career in jazz and am planning to relocate to the Los Angeles area in the very near future. I would be interested in learning more about the company and about available opportunities.

    I was a member of my high school jazz band for three years. In addition, I have been playing in the local coffee shop for the last two years. My demo CD, which is enclosed, contains three of my most requested songs.

    I would appreciate the opportunity to speak with you. Thank you for your time and consideration. I look forward to speaking with you about this exciting opportunity.

5. Press Enter three times, and type the closing Sincerely, Press enter four times, and type your name.

6. Insert a footer that contains the file name.

7. Delete the first instance of the word *very* in the second body paragraph, and insert the word modern in front of *jazz*.

Copyright © 2008 Pearson Prentice Hall   Page 1 of 1

Test Bank

Available as TestGen Software or as a Word document for customization.

Chapter 5: Creating Documents with Microsoft Word 2007

Multiple Choice:

1. With word processing programs, how are documents stored?

    A. On a network

    B. On the computer

    C. Electronically

    D. On the floppy disk

Answer: C   **Reference:** Objective 1: Create and Save a New Document   **Difficulty:** Moderate

2. Because you will see the document as it will print, _____ view is the ideal view to use when learning Microsoft Word 2007.

    A. Reading

    B. Normal

    C. Print Layout

    D. Outline

Answer: C   **Reference:** Objective 1: Create and Save a New Document   **Difficulty:** Moderate

3. The blinking vertical line where text or graphics will be inserted is called the:

    A. cursor.

    B. insertion point.

    C. blinking line.

    D. I-beam.

Answer: B   **Reference:** Objective 1: Create and Save a New Document   **Difficulty:** Easy

**Solution Files–
Application
and PDF
format**

Music School Records

Music School Records discovers, launches, and develops the careers of young artists in classical, jazz, and contemporary music. Our philosophy is to not only shape, distribute, and sell a music product, but to help artists create a career that can last a lifetime. Too often in the music industry, artists are forced to fit their music to a trend that is short-lived. Music School Records does not just follow trends, we take a long-term view of the music industry and help our artists develop a style and repertoire that is fluid and flexible and that will appeal to audiences for years and even decades.

The music industry is constantly changing, but over the last decade, the changes have been enormous. New forms of entertainment such as DVDs, video games, and the Internet mean there is more competition for the leisure dollar in the market. New technologies give consumers more options for buying and listening to music, and they are demanding high quality recordings. Young consumers are comfortable with technology and want the music they love when and where they want it, no matter where they are or what they are doing.

Music School Records embraces new technologies and the sophisticated market of young music lovers. We believe that providing high quality recordings of truly talented artists make for more discerning listeners who will cherish the gift of music for the rest of their lives. The expertise of Music School Records includes:

- Insight into our target market and the ability to reach the desired audience
- The ability to access all current sources of music income
- A management team with years of experience in music commerce
- Innovative business strategies and artist development plans
- Investment in technology infrastructure for high quality recordings and business services

pagexxxix_top.docx

Online Assessment and Training

myitlab is Prentice Hall's new performance-based solution that allows you to easily deliver outcomes-based courses on Microsoft Office 2007, with customized training and defensible assessment. Key features of myitlab include:

A *true* **"system" approach:** myitlab content is the same as in your textbook.
Project-based *and* **skills-based:** Students complete real-life assignments.
Advanced reporting *and* **gradebook**: These include student click stream data.
No **installation required:** myitlab is completely Web-based. You just need an Internet connection, small plug-in, and Adobe Flash Player.

Ask your Prentice Hall sales representative for a demonstration or visit:

www.prenhall.com/myitlab

chapterone

Basic Computer Concepts

OBJECTIVES

At the end of this chapter you will be able to:

1. Define Computer and Identify the Four Basic Computing Functions
2. Identify the Different Types of Computers
3. Describe Hardware Devices and Their Uses
4. Identify Types of Software and Their Uses
5. Describe Networks and Define Network Terms
6. Identify Safe Computing Practices

Introduction

Computers are an integral part of our lives. They are found in homes, offices, stores, hospitals, libraries, and many other places. Computers are part of cars and phones, and they enable you to access bank accounts from home, shop online, and quickly communicate with people around the world by means of e-mail and the Internet. It is difficult to find a business or occupation that doesn't rely on computers. Whether it's a truck driver who keeps an electronic travel log or a high-powered stockbroker who needs up-to-the-second market information, computers make these tasks easier, more efficient, and more accurate.

Computers are all around us, which makes it important to learn basic computing skills and gain the knowledge to be a responsible computer user. Knowing how to use a computer makes you ***computer fluent***.

This chapter looks at different types of computers and their functions. It discusses computer hardware and software and the benefits of networking. In addition, this chapter also discusses the importance of safe computing practices and the ways that you can protect your computer from various threats.

Objective 1
Define Computer and Identify the Four Basic Computing Functions

What are the benefits of using computers? Becoming computer fluent can benefit you in several ways. The most practical advantage of being computer fluent is that it makes employees more attractive to potential employers. In fact, many employers expect employees to have basic computer skills when they are hired. If you are knowledgeable about computers and their uses, it also makes you a better consumer. It is easier to select and purchase the right computer for your needs if you understand computer terminology and the components of a computer. In addition, if you have a basic understanding of today's technology, you can better understand and use *new* technologies.

What are the basic functions of a computer? A **computer** is a programmable electronic device that can input, process, output, and store data. A computer takes **data** and converts it into **information**. Many people use the words *data* and *information* interchangeably; however, they are different in computing and it is important to understand the distinction. Each piece of data entered into a computer represents a single fact or idea. Data can be a word, a number, a sound, or a picture.

Information is data that has been processed so that it can be presented in an organized and meaningful way. You might also think of data as pieces of a jigsaw puzzle and information as the finished puzzle. Putting the pieces of the puzzle together gives you the overall picture. For example, CIS 110, the letter B, and the names Amy and Stevens are pieces of data. Individually, these pieces of data seem meaningless. However, when processed, this data becomes the information on a grade report that indicates Amy Stevens received a grade of B in her CIS 110 class.

The four basic computer functions are also known as the **information processing cycle**. The functions are

- **Input**—The computer gathers data or allows a user to add data.

- **Process**—Data is converted into information.

- **Output**—The processed results are retrieved from the computer.

- **Storage**—Data or information is stored for future use.

In the grade report, the instructor used a computer to enter, or input, the students' grades into the school's computerized grading system. A computer then processed this data along with data for other classes the students might have taken. In the example, the student, Amy, then received a written record of her grade or she accessed it online. Either way, the grade report was output by the computer. In addition, her grades remain stored in the system so they can be used to generate her transcript or to determine her future grade point average as she continues to take classes.

Objective 2
Identify the Different Types of Computers

What are the different types of computers and what are they used for? Although computers come in a variety of sizes and shapes, the basic components required to complete the information-processing cycle must be present in them. In addition to microcomputers—the desktop and notebook computers and mobile devices that many of us are familiar with—there are also specialty computers, including servers, mainframes, supercomputers, and embedded computers.

Microcomputers

What are microcomputers? **Microcomputers** are classified as small, inexpensive computers designed for personal use and are the computers that most people typically use. Computers in this category range in size from large desktop systems to handheld devices that fit in your pocket. Some of the most common types of microcomputers include the following:

- *Desktop computers* are computers that sit on the desk, floor, table, or another flat surface and have a detachable keyboard, mouse, monitor, and possibly other pieces of equipment.

  Desktop computers generally fall into two main categories: PCs or Macs. The PC, or personal computer—originally referred to as the IBM personal computer—is now manufactured by a variety of companies including Hewlett-Packard, Dell, and Gateway. The Apple Macintosh computer, now known as Mac, can perform the same functions as the PC.

  Computer users have been in a long-running argument about which is better—PC or Mac? There are pros and cons to both types of computers, but in reality, both are good systems and the choice usually comes down to personal preference. The primary differences between the PC and the Mac relate to the different microprocessors and operating systems each one uses. The PC is typically used in a Microsoft Windows operating environment, and the Mac uses the Mac operating system. Although the PC and the Mac each process information differently, both can perform the same types of tasks. The PC has a larger market share among general computer users and in business settings, whereas the Mac is popular with graphic design professionals.

- *Notebook computers* give users the ability to take their computers with them, making their information portable or mobile. Originally referred to as "laptops," this term is slowly being phased out in favor of the more accurate notebook designation. Although smaller than a desktop computer, notebook computers are not meant to be used on your lap, due to the amount of heat they generate. Notebooks are designed to be portable and include a rechargeable battery to provide power, permitting them to be used in a variety of places. Averaging about 6 pounds, a notebook's size and weight can also limit its computing power. Notebooks typically have a built-in display screen, a keyboard, and a pointing device, although it is possible to connect them to detachable devices for more comfortable desktop use.

- **Tablet computers** might seem similar to notebooks; however, they have some special features that set them apart. Tablet computers weigh less than notebooks, averaging about 3 pounds. They also have a convertible screen that swivels, allowing the tablet to be used like a standard notebook computer in one position or like a clipboard in the second position. This "clipboard" aspect is how the tablet got its name. When used in the tablet configuration, the user can actually write directly on the screen using a special pen known as a **stylus**. Tablets use advanced handwriting-recognition technology to convert handwriting to digital text. Many also use speech-recognition technology, which enables the user to record discussions or lectures, for example, or to control the computer using voice commands.

- **Mobile devices** include items such as **personal digital assistants (PDAs)**, **handheld computers**, and **smartphones**. These devices originally varied in size and purpose, but they are all ultra-lightweight and portable. PDAs were initially designed to provide a convenient resource for maintaining an organized calendar and list of business and personal associates. Handheld computers enabled users to access personal productivity software and send e-mail over the Internet, while smartphones added Internet capability to the wireless communication aspects of cell phones.

The newest mobile devices, often referred to simply as "handhelds," combine the best features of each of these devices. Many handheld devices now include personal productivity software and enable the user to play music, take photos, make phone calls, and access the Internet. PDAs and handheld computers often use a stylus, which is a pointed device used to input information and access various features. However, it is not uncommon for these devices to use a small detachable keyboard for text and data entry. As the features of mobile devices continue to converge, permitting them to perform similar tasks, it becomes more difficult to differentiate between these handheld devices. Figure 1.1 identifies four different types of microcomputers.

Figure 1.1

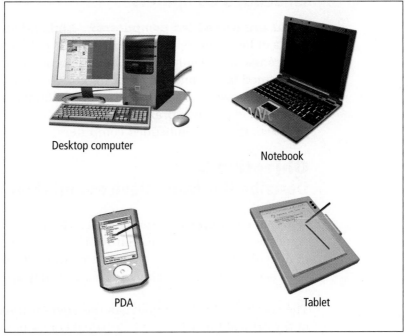

Desktop computer

Notebook

PDA

Tablet

Servers

What are servers?   **Servers** are an important component of computer networks. These specialized computers manage network resources through the use of administrative software, and they provide desktop computers with access to the network. Servers can handle a variety of resources or may be assigned to just one particular type of task. Thus, within the same company, you may find a Web server that processes requests for the organization's Web pages and a file server that handles the storage and retrieval tasks for all of the company's files stored on the network.

Mainframe Computers

What are mainframe computers?   **Mainframe computers** are large computers often found in businesses and colleges, where thousands of people are able to simultaneously use the computer to process data. Mainframe computers **multitask**; that is, they can perform more than one task at a time. Mainframes can store vast amounts of data using a variety of storage devices. Early mainframe computers were very large and required separate rooms to house them. Today's mainframe computers are significantly smaller.

Supercomputers

What are supercomputers?   **Supercomputers** are large, powerful computers that perform specialized tasks. You might have heard of Deep Blue, the IBM supercomputer that challenged champion chess players to chess matches—and beat them! Supercomputers are the fastest and most expensive computers. Unlike a mainframe computer that can handle a number of programs simultaneously, the supercomputer is designed to run fewer programs at one time, but to do so as quickly as possible. They perform sophisticated mathematical calculations, track weather patterns, monitor satellites, and perform other complex, dedicated tasks.

Embedded Computers

What are embedded computers?   **Embedded computers** are components of larger products that usually have a digital interface. These computers use a specially programmed microprocessor to perform a set of predefined tasks, and may require little or no input from the user. Microwave ovens, digital cameras, programmable thermostats, and airbags and antilock braking systems for cars are just a few examples of products that use embedded computers.

Objective 3
Describe Hardware Devices and Their Uses

What is computer hardware?   **Hardware** is the computer and any equipment connected to it. Hardware devices are the physical components of the computer. Items such as the monitor, keyboard, mouse, and printer are also known as **peripherals** because they attach to the computer.

The computer itself is known as the **system unit**, and it contains many of the critical hardware and electrical components. The system unit is sometimes referred to as the tower, box, or console. When the system unit is combined with the appropriate peripheral devices, the system can perform the four basic computer functions: input, process, output, and storage. Peripheral devices are used to input and output data and information, and the system unit processes and stores the data. Figure 1.2 shows a standard computer system and identifies the function each piece of hardware performs.

Figure 1.2

System Unit

What is inside the system unit? If you remove the cover from the system unit, you find several key components inside. One of the most essential components is the **microprocessor chip**, also known as the **central processing unit (CPU)**. The CPU is located on the **motherboard**, a large printed circuit board to which all the other circuit boards in the computer are connected. Figure 1.3 displays a standard motherboard and identifies its components. The table in Figure 1.4 identifies and explains each of the components.

Figure 1.3

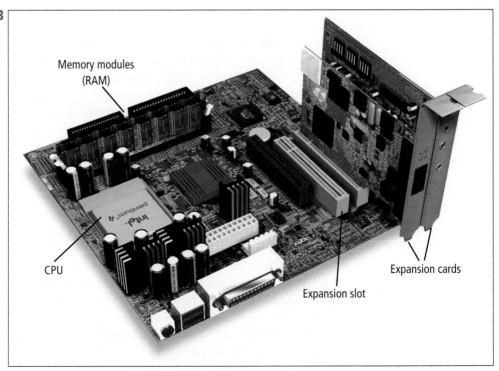

Motherboard Features

Component	Description
Motherboard/System board	The main computer circuit board that connects all computer components.
CPU	The central processing unit that gets data from memory and performs mathematical or logical operations to process the data.
Memory (RAM) chips	The temporary holding area inside the computer where data is stored electronically to make it accessible for processing. Data must be stored in memory, so the processor can access and process it. RAM stands for Random Access Memory.
Memory (RAM) slots	The slots on the motherboard used to hold memory (RAM) chips.
Expansion cards	Removable circuit boards used to add new peripherals or increase computer capabilities.
Expansion slots	The slots used to hold expansion cards.

Figure 1.4

What does the CPU do? The CPU is the brain of the computer, and is responsible for controlling the commands and tasks that the computer performs. It has two main parts—the **control unit** and the **arithmetic logic unit (ALU)**. The control unit is responsible for obtaining instructions from the computer's memory. It then interprets these instructions and executes them, thereby coordinating the activities of all the other computer components. The arithmetic logic unit, or ALU, performs all the arithmetic and logic functions for the computer. The ALU handles addition, subtraction, multiplication, and division, and also makes logical and comparison decisions. This enables the CPU to perform tasks such as sorting data alphabetically or numerically and filtering data to locate specific criteria.

As important as the CPU is to your computer, you might expect it to take up a large amount of space in the console. However, the CPU is actually rather small. Over the years, manufacturers have successfully attempted to reduce the size of microprocessor chips while continuing to increase their computing power. In fact, Moore's law (formulated in 1965 by Gordon Moore, cofounder of Intel) addresses this increase in computing power, observing that current production methods allow CPU capacity to double every 18 months!

Are there different brands of CPUs? The most well-known chip manufacturers include Intel, Advanced Micro Devices (AMD), and Motorola. Chip manufacturers often produce several different models of chips. Some of the chips that Intel makes include Core Duo, Pentium, Celeron, and Centrino. AMD manufactures chips such as the Athlon, Sempron, and Turion. Intel and AMD chips are the mainstays for PCs. For many years, Apple relied on Motorola to provide the PowerPC processor, the only CPUs the Macintosh used. However, in 2006, Apple stopped producing PowerPC-based systems and began using Intel chips, such as the Core Duo, in its computers.

How is a CPU's processing power measured? One indicator of a CPU's processing power is its ***clock speed***. Clock speed measures the speed at which a CPU processes data and is measured in ***megahertz (MHz)*** or ***gigahertz (GHz)***, depending on the age of the CPU. Early computers had CPUs that processed at speeds of less than 5 MHz, whereas modern processors can operate at over 3 GHz (the equivalent of 3,000 MHz) and newer processors continue to surpass these numbers.

Are there other factors that affect a CPU's processing power? CPUs may use different technologies to enhance their processing performance. Some Intel chips use ***hyperthreading*** technology, which enables the microprocessor to act as if it were two processors, resulting in faster processing and improved processing power. ***Dual-core*** or ***multicore*** processors are manufactured by Intel and AMD. These CPUs have more than one processor (two for a dual-core, more for a multicore) on a single chip. Using multiple processors has several advantages over a single processor CPU, including improved multitasking capabilities and system performance, lower power consumption, reduced usage of system resources, and lower heat emissions.

What types of memory does a computer have and what are they used for? Memory is another critical computer component found within the system unit. There are two basic types of memory: ROM and RAM. ***ROM***, or ***Read Only Memory***, is prerecorded on a chip. As the name implies, the computer can read this memory, although that's all it can do. The information on a ROM chip can't be changed, removed, or rewritten and is generally inaccessible to the computer user. ROM is also known as ***nonvolatile*** memory because it retains its contents even if the computer is turned off. ROM is used to store critical information, such as the program used to start up, or ***boot***, the computer.

The second type of memory is ***RAM***, which stands for ***Random Access Memory***. RAM acts as the computer's short-term memory and stores data temporarily as it is being processed. RAM is considered to be ***volatile*** because this memory is erased when the computer is turned off. The more tasks your computer performs at the same time, the more memory is used.

Why is it important to have enough RAM? Your computer's RAM is like the juggler for your system. When you first start your computer, it's as if a juggler is tossing bean bags. As you open more programs, or use a memory-intensive program such as a video editor, the level of difficulty for the juggler increases. Soon RAM is trying to juggle the equivalent of bowling balls! If you don't have a sufficient amount of memory in your system, you might notice your computer slows down or even stops responding if you try to do too much at one time. Computer users often think this means they have too much information saved on their computer's hard drive. It really means that they are running out of memory, not storage space. To fix this problem, you can reduce the number of programs running at the same time or you can add more RAM to your system.

Installing new memory is one of the cheapest and easiest upgrades you can do for your computer and often results in noticeable performance improvements. RAM is usually measured in **megabytes (MB)** or **gigabytes (GB)**. For newer systems, a minimum of 512 MB to 1 GB is recommended. If you are thinking of purchasing a new computer, experts recommend you buy one with as much RAM as possible.

Storage Devices

What are storage devices?   Storage devices are used to store the data and information used by or created with the computer. Such storage is often referred to as **permanent memory** because, unlike data that is in RAM, data saved to a storage device remains there until the user deletes or overwrites it. Data can be stored within internal hardware devices located within the system unit or in removable external units. Additionally, storage can be fixed or portable, depending on whether the data saved remains within the system unit or is saved on removable units and accessed elsewhere.

How is data stored?   Before discussing specific storage devices, it is helpful to understand the different technologies used to store data. Data is generally saved using one of three forms of storage medium: magnetic, optical, or flash memory.

- **Magnetic** storage uses tape or film covered in a thin, magnetic coating that enables data to be saved as magnetic particles. It works in much the same fashion as an audiocassette or videotape works. Hard disks, floppy disks, Zip disks, and backup tape are all forms of magnetic media. Magnetic disks are divided into **tracks** and **sectors**. Just like an old vinyl record, tracks form rings around the circumference of the media. Sectors divide the tracks into pie-shaped wedges extending from the center to the outer edge of the disk. Data is stored magnetically within the sectors. Magnetic media has read/write capability, which means it is possible to use it over and over again, enabling you to delete or revise existing data and save new data.

- **Optical** storage uses flat plastic discs coated in a special reflective material. Data is saved by using a laser beam to burn tiny pits into the storage medium. The laser is also used to read the saved data. The saved data is organized using tracks and sectors, similar to those used in magnetic media. Compact discs (CDs) and digital video discs (DVDs) are examples of optical media. Unlike magnetic media, not all optical storage is read/write capable. CD-ROMs and DVD-ROMs are considered read-only media (ROM); the information contained on them can be read, but not changed or deleted, and it is not possible to save new data to them. If you purchase new software, music, or a movie, it is most likely on a CD-ROM or DVD-ROM. A record-only disc, or CD-R, allows you to record, or **burn**, information to the disc one time only; information saved this way cannot be deleted or rewritten. A rewritable disc, known as a CD-RW, allows information to be recorded, revised, or deleted, and new data can also be written to the disc, just as with magnetic media. The same possibilities are available in DVDs. However, there are currently two competing formats—DVD-R/RW, known as "DVD dash," and DVD+R/RW, known as "DVD plus." The R/RW suffix indicates the DVD can be used to record and can also be rewritten. Although most DVD players can play either format, if you want to record to a DVD, you need to know which format the DVD recorder requires.

- **Flash memory** uses solid-state technology. It is completely electronic and has no moving mechanical parts. Flash memory is a quick and easy form of rewritable storage, capable of exceeding the storage capacity of magnetic or optical media. Flash memory cards are often used in mobile devices such as PDAs, digital cameras, and MP3 players. Depending on the manufacturer, flash memory cards may be called Memory Stick, CompactFlash, Secure Digital, or MultiMediaCard. Typically, a device can use only one style of memory card; however, a computer equipped with the appropriate card reader can read any of them. Small, removable storage devices known as flash drives also use flash technology and have become increasingly popular.

The table in Figure 1.5 lists the various types of storage media and their capacities.

Figure 1.5

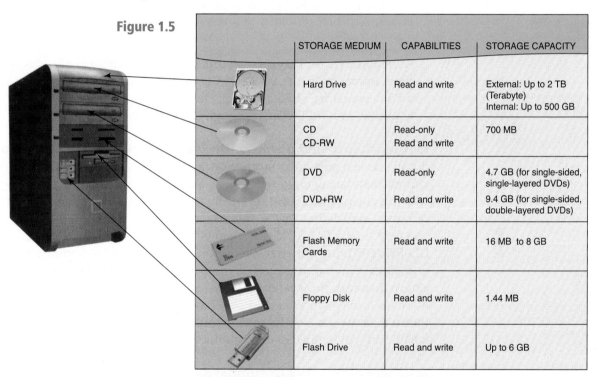

	STORAGE MEDIUM	CAPABILITIES	STORAGE CAPACITY
	Hard Drive	Read and write	External: Up to 2 TB (Terabyte) Internal: Up to 500 GB
	CD CD-RW	Read-only Read and write	700 MB
	DVD DVD+RW	Read-only Read and write	4.7 GB (for single-sided, single-layered DVDs) 9.4 GB (for single-sided, double-layered DVDs)
	Flash Memory Cards	Read and write	16 MB to 8 GB
	Floppy Disk	Read and write	1.44 MB
	Flash Drive	Read and write	Up to 6 GB

What are the main types of storage devices? Depending on the age and type of computer you have, you might find some or all of the following internal storage options:

- **Hard disk drive**—A hard disk drive is the computer's largest internal storage device. Also referred to as a hard drive, its storage space is usually measured in gigabytes (GB), with newer computers ranging in size from 40 GB to 500 GB, although it is possible to find some specialized, high-end computers with storage space measuring up to 2 terabytes (TB). As with everything else in computing, these numbers tend to increase with each new model. Hard drives are traditionally permanent storage devices fixed inside the system unit.

- **Floppy disk drive**—The floppy disk drive was the original storage device for microcomputers. Floppy disks are magnetic media capable of holding up to 1.44 megabytes (MB) of data, and are an example of portable storage. Although floppy disks are still a viable storage method for small, text-based files, their limited capacity makes them ill-suited for larger graphics or multimedia files. They can be useful for saving and transporting small files, or backing up individual files for safekeeping. Floppy drives are considered legacy technology and many newer computers no longer include them as standard equipment, primarily because other higher-capacity storage methods are beginning to replace this old standby. If you can't live without one, it might be possible to special order a floppy drive if you purchase a customized computer or to install one after the fact.

- **CD and/or DVD drives**—Your computer may have one, two, or none of these optical drives. As a general rule, new computers come equipped with at least a CD drive to provide an option for portable storage. It's important to know whether this drive is a simple CD-ROM drive, which can only read CDs, or if it is a CD-RW drive, also known as a CD burner. A **CD burner** gives you the ability to save, or burn, files to a CD. You might also have a separate drive that can read and/or write DVDs. Another configuration is to have only one optical drive: a CD-RW/DVD drive.

  Although CDs and DVDs look alike, DVDs are capable of holding much more information than CDs. A CD can hold up to 700 MB of data, but a DVD can store almost 10 GB! Because of their differences, a CD drive is unable to read DVDs, although a DVD drive can read CDs.

Is it possible to add a storage device to a system? If your system doesn't have a particular storage device, it may be possible to add it—if your system has enough room for it. You would need an available drive bay, which is the physical location within the system unit, or you might consider removing an existing device and replacing it with another. For instance, if you only have a CD-ROM drive you could remove that and replace it with a CD-RW/DVD drive, thereby giving you the ability to read and burn CDs and play DVDs too. It is also possible to purchase many of these units as external storage devices. An external storage device is a peripheral that attaches to the computer and performs the same tasks as its corresponding internal device. One of the most popular of these is the external hard drive, which can greatly increase a computer's storage capacity.

Are there other types of storage devices? Other storage devices you might be familiar with include **flash drives**, a newer form of data storage, as well as two older, legacy drives—**Zip drives** and **backup tape drives**.

- **Flash drives** are removable storage devices that use flash memory and connect to the computer by a USB port. Flash drives are also known as thumb drives, universal serial bus (USB) drives, and jump drives. The flash drive is typically a device small enough to fit on a keychain or in a pocket and, because of its solid-state circuitry and lack of moving parts, it is extremely durable. Available in several storage sizes ranging from 16 MB to 64 GB, a flash drive is a quick and easy way to save and transport files. As an example, a 64-MB flash drive, which is relatively small, holds the equivalent of almost 45 floppy disks! To use one of these devices, you simply plug it into a computer's USB port. The computer recognizes the new device and enables the user to save or retrieve files from the flash drive.

- **Zip drives** are magnetic storage devices that save data to Zip disks. Zip disks appear similar to floppy disks but are capable of holding 100 MB, 250 MB, or 750 MB of information. Some older computers may include an internal Zip drive, but they are more often found as external storage devices. Zip drives were popular in earlier computers, but they are rarely found in newer models because they have been replaced by the more efficient and affordable optical and flash drives.

- **Backup tape drives** are storage devices that resemble audiocassette tape recorders and save data to magnetic tape. Although they are rarely used for home computers anymore, many businesses and organizations still rely on tape backup systems to safeguard their data on a daily basis.

The capacity of the components found in your system unit is measured in terms of storage size or speed. Computer systems continue to increase in storage capacity and computing speed, while decreasing in size. Generally, higher measurements indicate a system that is quicker and more powerful than a system with lower measurements. However, it is important to balance size and speed with financial considerations too. Although it is tempting to consider buying a computer with the most power possible, a lesser computer may be more reasonably priced and still be sufficient for the typical user's needs. Recall that CPU speed is measured in megahertz (MHz) or gigahertz (GHz). The amount of RAM in a computer is generally measured in megabytes (MB), while storage space is usually measured in megabytes or gigabytes (GB), depending on the device. Figure 1.6 illustrates an explanation of the various measurements and how they relate to each other.

Evaluating Your System

Now that you have seen some of the items you can find in a computer, you might wonder about your computer's features. If you're new to computers, you might not know all the details about your computer, especially if you didn't buy it brand new. If you did buy a new computer, the easiest way is to check your paperwork—all the basic information should be there. However, if your computer isn't new or you didn't keep the paperwork, there are some ways to determine exactly what is in your system.

What kind of computer do you have?   This is one of the easiest questions to answer. Like almost every other appliance you've used, you can probably find the manufacturer's name and a brand name or model number on the case of the computer. If not, check the back of the unit; there should be a metal tag that will include the manufacturer name, model number, and serial number.

What operating system does the computer use?   If you watch carefully as a computer boots up, you can often determine the operating system. If the computer uses Microsoft Windows, you will usually see a splash screen display for a few moments, showing the version of Windows that is running (for example, Windows 95, Windows 98, Windows Me, Windows XP, Windows Vista, and so on).

How much memory is in the computer?   What is the type and speed of the CPU?   To determine how much memory or RAM is

How Much Is a Byte?

Name	Abbreviation	Number of Bytes	Relative Size
Byte	B	1 byte	Can hold one character of data.
Kilobyte	KB	1,024 bytes	Can hold 1,024 characters or about half of a typewritten page double-spaced.
Megabyte	MB	1,048,576 bytes	A floppy disk holds approximately 1.4 MB of data, or approximately 768 pages of typed text.
Gigabyte	GB	1,073,741,824 bytes	Approximately 786,432 pages of text. Because 500 sheets of paper is approximately 2 inches, this represents a stack of paper 262 feet high.
Terabyte	TB	1,099,511,627,776 bytes	This represents a stack of typewritten pages almost 51 miles high.
Petabyte	PB	1,125,899,906,842,624 bytes	The stack of pages is now 52,000 miles high, or about one-fourth the distance from the Earth to the moon.

Figure 1.6

installed, or which model and type of CPU is in the system, locate the My Computer icon on your desktop and right-click it. Select Properties from the resulting shortcut menu. As you see in Figure 1.7, the General tab of the System Properties dialog box provides a lot of information about your system. This view shows you the operating system used on the computer, which is helpful if you didn't see the splash screen at startup, and also to whom the system is registered. Additionally, you can determine the computer manufacturer and model name, the type of CPU and its chip speed, and the amount of memory or RAM that is installed.

In Figure 1.7, the computer shown is running Windows XP Home Edition with Service Pack 2 installed. It has an Intel Pentium 4 chip, with a speed of 1,600 MHz, which is equivalent to 1.60 GHz. In addition, this system has 512 MB of RAM.

Figure 1.7

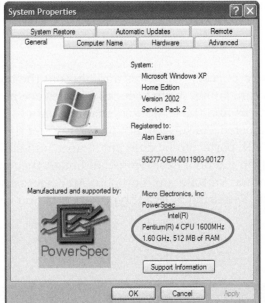

How do you determine what drives are on the system and how much storage space is available? It's important to know how much information you can store on your computer and how much room you have left. Is there enough storage space or is the computer getting full? Use My Computer to find the answers. Double-click the My Computer icon on the desktop to open a dialog box that displays your hard disk drive (or drives), in addition to all the removable storage devices attached to your system. For more information about your hard drive (or any other storage device), choose the drive you want to look at, and then right-click. Click Properties from the resulting menu. A new dialog box displays, similar to the one shown in Figure 1.8. The pie chart displayed on

Figure 1.8

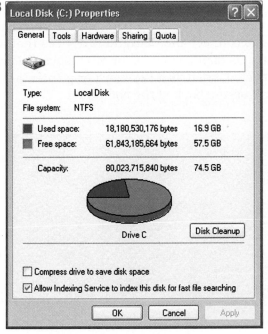

the General tab is a good visual tool that shows the size of your hard drive and how much space is in use.

Ports

What are ports? The wires and plugs at the back of a computer can seem intimidating. A **port** acts as an interface between a system's peripheral devices and the computer, enabling data to be exchanged once they are connected. As you can see on the back of the notebook shown in Figure 1.9, ports can be different shapes and sizes. The same ports are typically found on a desktop too, although they might be arranged in a different order. Various input and output devices use different data exchange methods, requiring different types of ports and connectors (or plugs).

Figure 1.9

USB ports
FireWire port
Modem port or RJ-11 port

DVI port
Parallel port
Monitor port
S-video
Speaker port
Microphone port
Ethernet port

How do you determine which port a peripheral device needs? Manufacturers have attempted to make the process of connecting peripheral devices less complicated on newer computers. Rather than trying to match the size and shape of a connector to its port, many manufacturers now use a color-coding system that coordinates the colors of the connectors with their corresponding ports. Additionally, many newer desktop computers include ports, such as USB and audio ports, on the front panel of the system unit to provide easier access to them, as shown in Figure 1.10. Locating these ports on the front panel makes it a simple process to connect and disconnect devices that are used only occasionally, such as digital cameras or MP3 players. Peripherals that are rarely disconnected, such as a keyboard or printer, are generally plugged into the ports on the back of the computer.

Figure 1.10

Audio ports
FireWire port
USB ports

What are the different ports used for? Serial and parallel ports are two of the oldest types of ports found on a computer. **Serial ports** are ports that can send data only one bit at a time, so the data exchange rate is slow compared to newer technology. The maximum rate at which a standard serial port can transfer data is 115 kilobits per second (Kbps). The mouse and modem are examples of devices that might use a serial port. A **parallel port** is a port that sends data in groups of bits, at transfer rates of up to 500 Kbps, so it is a considerably faster method of transferring data than the serial port. Older printers were often connected to a computer through a parallel port.

Are there faster ports? Over the years, newer ports have come into existence. One of these is the **universal serial bus (USB) port**. This type of port is able to interface with several different peripheral devices, which reduces the need for individual, dedicated ports. USB ports are also able to transfer data at extremely high rates of speed. Original USB ports, known as USB 1.1, are capable of speeds of 12 megabits per second (Mbps). The newest version, USB 2.0, can attain a rate of 480 Mbps—40 times faster than USB 1.1 technology and over 400 times faster than a serial port! USB 2.0 ports are backwards compatible, which means that older USB devices work with them, however, data will only transfer at the slower USB 1.1 speed. The higher data transfer capabilities of USB ports, coupled with their capability to work with multiple devices, have made the older serial and parallel ports obsolete. Because of the USB port's speedy data transfer rate and its ability to be used with numerous devices, new computers often include four or more USB ports. Devices using USB ports include keyboards, mice, printers, MP3 players, and PDAs. In general, it's a good idea to get a computer with as many USB ports as possible.

The **FireWire port**, developed by Apple and also known as IEEE 1394, is another means of transferring data quickly. The FireWire 400 has a data transfer rate of 400 Mbps, while the newer FireWire 800 transfers data at a blazing 800 Mbps! This port is typically used to connect devices that need to transfer huge amounts of data to a computer quickly, such as digital cameras or digital video recorders, or external hard drives. FireWire ports are standard on many Apple products, but are usually found only on higher-end Windows PCs and peripheral devices. Some peripheral devices offer users a choice of connecting using a USB port or a FireWire port.

What kind of port is used to connect to another computer?
Connectivity ports, such as Ethernet and modem ports, are used to connect a computer to a local network or to the Internet. An **Ethernet port**, also known as an RJ-45 jack, resembles a standard phone jack, but is slightly larger. The Ethernet port is used for network access and can also be used to connect a cable modem or router for Internet access. A **modem port** is the same size and shape as a phone jack and is used to connect the modem to a phone system, enabling dial-up Internet access. The maximum data transfer rate for a modem is 56 Kbps, while the most common Ethernet standard, Fast Ethernet, transfers data at the rate of 100 Mbps. However, Gigabit Ethernet, with a potential transfer rate of 1,000 Mbps, is becoming an option on higher-end systems, and is standard on many Mac systems.

Even faster Ethernet technologies, such as 10 Gigabit Ethernet or 10GbE, exist, but they are currently used for network backbones and enterprise network infrastructures, rather than home users. The table in Figure 1.11 lists some of the different types of ports and the devices that use them.

Ports and Their Uses

Port Name	Port Shape	Connector Shape	Data Transfer Speed	Typical Devices Attached to Port
Legacy Technologies				
Serial			115 Kbps	Mice External modems
Parallel	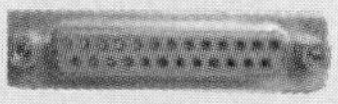		500 Kbps	Printers External Zip drives
USB 1.1			12 Mbps	Mice Keyboards External Zip drives Printers Scanners Game controllers
New Technologies				
USB 2.0			480 Mbps	Same as USB 1.1, but at faster transfer rates Also suitable for camcorders and digital cameras Maintains backward compatibility with USB 1.1
FireWire/ FireWire 800			400 Mbps/ 800 Mbps	Digital video camcorders Digital cameras
Ethernet/ Gigabit Ethernet			Up to 100 Mbps/ Up to 1,000 Mbps	Network connections Cable modems

Figure 1.11

Are there special purpose ports? Despite the prevalence of USB ports, which can be used for a variety of peripherals, there are still some devices that require special ports. These ports include Musical Instrument Digital Interface (MIDI), IrDA, Bluetooth, video, and audio ports:

- ***MIDI ports*** are used to connect electronic musical devices, such as keyboards and synthesizers, to a computer, enabling musicians to create digital music files.

- The **IrDA port** is used to allow devices such as PDAs, keyboards, mice, and printers to transmit data wirelessly to another device by using infrared light waves. In order to transmit information, each of the devices must have an IrDA port, as well as a clear line of sight, with no other objects blocking the transmission.

- **Bluetooth** is another type of wireless technology that relies on radio wave transmission and doesn't require a clear line of sight. Bluetooth-enabled devices such as PDAs or other mobile devices can only communicate with each other over short distances, typically less than 30 feet.

- Video ports include standard monitor ports, DVI ports, and S-video ports. A **monitor port** is used to connect the monitor to the graphics processing unit, which is usually located on the motherboard or on a video card. However, to get the best results from a flat panel (LCD) monitor, the **Digital Video Interface (DVI) port** should be used instead. The DVI port transmits a pure digital signal, eliminating the need for digital-to-analog conversion and resulting in a higher quality transmission and a clearer picture on the monitor. The **S-video port** is typically used to connect other video sources, such as a television, projector, or digital recorder, to the computer.

- Similar to video ports, **audio ports** connect audio devices, such as speakers, headphones, and microphones, to the computer's sound card. These jacks will probably be very familiar to anyone who is accustomed to using standard stereo components.

Input Devices

The system unit and its storage devices process and store data. However, before that can happen, you need to get the data into the system. You also need a way to get the processed data back out of the system. **Input** and **output devices** are used to enter and retrieve the data in a useful format.

The two most familiar input devices are the keyboard and the mouse, but they aren't the only ones. This section discusses each of these devices, in addition to some other useful devices used to get data into the computer.

Keyboards

Are there different types of keyboards? The **keyboard** is the primary input device for computers. There are actually several different kinds of keyboards. The QWERTY keyboard is the one most people are familiar with. It is based on the original typewriter keyboard and is named for the arrangement of the letters on the top-left alphabetic row of keys. Another style is the Dvorak keyboard, which arranges the letters and numbers in a different pattern for increased typing speed. Some ergonomic keyboards use a split keyboard arrangement, offsetting each half at an angle to reduce the incidence of repetitive stress injuries such as carpal tunnel syndrome.

Keyboard size and layout on notebook and tablet computers can differ slightly from a standard desktop keyboard. Keyboards usually send information to the computer through a cable connected to a USB port; however, wireless or remote keyboards are gaining in popularity. A wireless keyboard communicates with the computer by infrared or radio frequency technology and also requires batteries.

What are all these other keys used for? In addition to the standard alphanumeric keys originally found on typewriters, computer keyboards have a variety of keys that provide additional functionality. Many of these keys are shown in Figure 1.12 and include

- ***Control keys***, such as the Ctrl, Alt, and Windows keys, often provide shortcuts or increased functionality to the keyboard when used in combination with another key. If you press the Shift key and a letter, the result is an uppercase, rather than a lowercase, letter. In the same way, using one of the control keys enables the standard keys to be used for additional purposes. For example, pressing Ctrl and the letter P opens the Print dialog box. Another example of a control key is the Esc key, which can often be used to stop, or *escape*, from a currently running task. A unique control key that is found only on Windows-based keyboards is the Windows key.

- The ***numeric keypad***, located at the right of the keyboard, provides an alternate method of quickly entering numbers. This is useful for individuals who are accustomed to using an adding machine or calculator.

- ***Function keys*** are located above the standard row of number keys. Numbered F1 through F12, these keys are generally associated with certain software-specific commands. Pressing the F1 key will usually open the Help menu for a program; however, pressing one of the other function keys can produce different results, depending on the software program running.

- ***Arrow keys*** are the keys located at the bottom of the keyboard between the standard keys and the numeric keypad. These keys enable the user to move the insertion point around the window one space at a time.

- ***Toggle and other keys***, which are located just above the arrow keys, are used for various purposes, including navigation and editing. The Insert, Num Lock, and Caps Lock keys are all examples of toggle keys. A toggle key works just like a light switch—press it once and the feature is turned on, press it again and it is turned off. If you've ever accidentally pressed the Caps Lock key and typed a long string of all capital letters, you've seen this feature in action. Pressing the Caps Lock key again allows you to return to normal keyboarding mode.

- ***Multimedia and Internet control keys*** are typically found at the top edge of the keyboard. The precise placement and function of these keys usually depends on the keyboard manufacturer. However, most modern keyboards have at least a few keys or buttons that can be used for such tasks as muting or adjusting speaker volume, opening a Web browser, and sending an e-mail. Generally, each button has an icon that indicates its function.

Figure 1.12

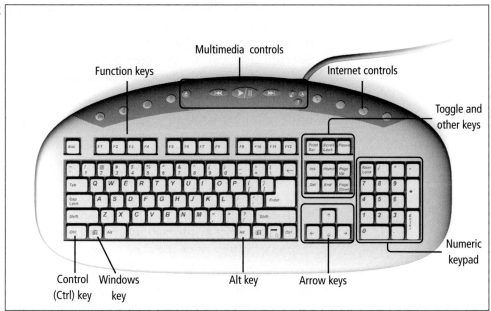

The Mouse

Is there an easier way to control cursor movement? The ***mouse*** became an essential input device with the introduction of graphical user interfaces, such as Microsoft Windows. This point-and-click device is useful for positioning the insertion point by translating hand movements into corresponding actions on the screen. If the mouse has a rollerball on the bottom, you also need a mousepad to create the friction necessary for the mouse to track properly. Optical mice use a laser beam, instead of a rollerball, to control the pointer movement. Because the bottom of an optical mouse is sealed, dirt and debris are less likely to get inside and interfere with the mouse's internal mechanisms. Such mice don't require mousepads, although many people continue to use one. Just as with keyboards, mice can be wired or wireless. Notebook and tablet computers can use mice, or they may use a built-in touchpad, trackball, or trackpoint to move the insertion point.

How can the mouse be used more efficiently? Although there are different kinds of mice, the traditional mouse has two buttons and a scroll wheel. The palm of your hand should rest comfortably over the mouse. For the best and most accurate results when you click the mouse, simply press the button with your finger. Often, people who are new to computing think they need to lift their finger and press hard to click a mouse button. This can actually create problems by causing the mouse to move suddenly, making clicking inaccurate. The following provides a brief description of some of the ways the mouse can be used:

- ***Click***—By default, the left mouse button is considered the primary button. When instructed to click the mouse, it is understood this means that the left mouse button should be pressed one time. Clicking is done to position the insertion point or to select an object on the screen.

- **Double-click**—Double-clicking is performed by pressing the left mouse button two times in rapid succession. It is important that the mouse does not move while double-clicking or the command will not produce the expected results. Double-clicking is done to activate an object; for example, you double-click to open a file or start a program.

- **Drag**—To carry out this action, press the left mouse button and continue to hold it while dragging, or moving, the mouse. This action can be used to select large blocks of text.

- **Right-click**—Pressing the right mouse button one time will open a shortcut menu. Shortcut menus are usually context-sensitive, which means they will vary depending on what you've clicked and what program you are using. The right mouse button is also known as the secondary button and is not typically pressed more than one time—no double-clicking for the right button. After the shortcut menu has been opened, you select the appropriate choice by clicking it with the left mouse button.

- **Scroll wheel**—If your mouse is equipped with a scroll wheel, it can be used to quickly move a page up or down in a window. It is an easy way to navigate through lengthy documents or Web sites.

Are there other input devices? Although the keyboard and mouse are the two most common input devices, there are many other input devices. **Scanners** are similar to copy machines, but instead of producing a paper copy, they convert documents or photos to digital files that can then be saved on your computer. **Microphones** are used to digitally record sounds. Game controls such as **joysticks** are used to control movement within games. **Digital cameras** and **digital video recorders** enable you to transfer digital images of photos and movies directly to your computer.

Output Devices

Output devices help you retrieve data that has been entered, processed, and stored in your system and present it in a useful format. This format can be text, graphics, audio, or video. Monitors and printers are the two most common output devices.

Monitors

What are monitors? **Monitors**, also known as **display screens**, are an essential component of the computer system. Text, video, and graphics are displayed on a monitor. When a monitor outputs data or information, it is called **soft copy**—you can view it, but you can't touch it.

What is the difference between a CRT monitor and an LCD monitor?
Monitors come in a variety of sizes and styles, but, as shown in Figure 1.13, there are just two main categories: **cathode-ray tube (CRT)** and **liquid crystal display (LCD)**. A CRT monitor resembles a traditional television set and uses a cathode-ray tube to produce the picture on the screen. The glass screen of a CRT monitor can be curved or flat (sometimes called a **flat screen** monitor). The flat screen generally has less glare. It is important not to confuse a flat screen monitor with a flat panel monitor. **Flat panel** or LCD monitors use a liquid crystal display and are much thinner and lighter than CRT monitors. They are also more expensive than CRTs, although they have become more affordable in recent years.

Figure 1.13

What factors determine a monitor's display quality? A monitor's display is made up of millions of tiny dots, known as ***pixels***. Each pixel, which is short for picture element, represents a single point on a display screen or in a graphic image. The number of pixels on the screen determines a monitor's sharpness and clarity, also known as its ***resolution***. A higher number of pixels results in a clearer and sharper monitor resolution. A standard screen resolution might be expressed as 1024 x 768, which means there are 1,024 columns, each containing 768 pixels, for a total of more than 786,000 pixels on the screen.

Dot pitch is another display characteristic and refers to the diagonal distance between two pixels of the same color. Dot pitch is measured in millimeters with smaller measurements resulting in a crisper viewing image because there is less blank space between the pixels. For best viewing, monitors should have a dot pitch measurement of .28 mm or less. CRT monitors use an electric beam to light up the pixels. The electric beam quickly passes back and forth across the back of the screen, relighting the pixels and redrawing the screen image. LCD monitors use an electric current to illuminate the pixels. The speed at which the pixels are reilluminated is called the ***refresh rate***, which is measured in cycles per second, expressed as hertz (Hz). Refresh rates generally average between 75 and 85 Hz, which means the screen image is redrawn 75 to 85 times per second. Higher refresh rates result in less screen flicker and less eye strain.

How are a monitor's color settings and display size determined? Although monochrome monitors were the standard in the early days of computers, color monitors are more common now. Modern monitors can display at least 256 colors and most can display up to 16.8 million colors. Monitor sizes range from 14 to 40 inches or larger. Desktop computers use CRT or LCD monitors, whereas notebook and tablet computers use LCD screens. Popular desktop sizes include 17-inch, 19-inch, and 21-inch monitors. Notebooks tend to have slightly smaller LCD screens, which range from 12 to 17 inches. Monitor sizes are determined by measuring them diagonally. However, the measurement for a CRT monitor includes the outer housing, which makes the actual viewing area of the monitor smaller than the size indicated. LCD monitor measurements do not include the bezel, or edge, of the screen. Because of these different measurement methods, a 17-inch LCD monitor has virtually the same viewing area as a 19-inch CRT monitor.

Which type of monitor is best? Consider some of the following questions to help make your decision. How much can you afford to spend? Do you have the room for a CRT monitor or is your workspace limited? How important is color accuracy to you or your work?

There are advantages and disadvantages to both types of monitors, and the ultimate decision should be based on which one will work best for you. CRT monitors are cheaper and tend to display colors better; however, LCD monitors are becoming less expensive. LCD monitors are also smaller and lighter weight, with a larger display screen than similarly sized CRTs. Figure 1.14 compares the advantages for both CRT and LCD monitors to help you decide which style best suits your needs.

CRT Monitors Versus LCD Monitors

CRT Monitor Advantages	LCD Monitor Advantages
Images viewable from all angles (LCD monitors often have a limited viewing angle).	Take up less space and weigh less.
Resolution can be adjusted more completely.	Cause less eye strain than CRT monitors.
Better color accuracy and clarity.	Are more environmentally friendly than CRT monitors.
Better for gaming and watching DVDs due to quicker pixel response time and higher color accuracy than LCD monitors.	Larger viewable area compared with similar sized CRT (17-inch viewable area on 17-inch monitor compared with 15-inch viewable area on a 17-inch CRT monitor).

Figure 1.14

Printers

Using a monitor is a good way to view the information on your computer, but sometimes a soft copy isn't sufficient for your needs. The ability to generate a **hard copy**—a permanent record of your work—is the primary benefit of a **printer**.

What types of printers are available? There are two categories of printers: impact and nonimpact. **Impact** printers have small keys, similar to a typewriter's, that strike an ink ribbon against paper, leaving behind an image of the character on the key. The **dot matrix** printer is an impact printer. One of the earliest printers, the dot matrix printer has been almost completely phased out by newer types of printers. Despite this, the dot matrix printer can still be found in some business settings because it is useful for printing multipage forms such as invoices or purchase orders.

How does a nonimpact printer work? **Nonimpact** printers do not actually touch the paper when printing. There are a variety of nonimpact printers, but the two most commonly used with home computers are the ink-jet printer and the laser printer. Figure 1.15 shows a typical example of each of these printers. The *ink-jet* printer uses a special nozzle and ink cartridges to spray ink in small droplets onto the surface of the paper. Ink-jet printers are able to easily print in color and in black and white, produce good quality copy, and are relatively inexpensive to buy. *Laser* printers use the same process as photocopiers to produce their output. They use a special cylinder known as a drum, dry ink or toner, and a laser. Static electricity attracts toner to the surface of the drum and the laser distributes the toner in the correct pattern. The drum transfers the toner to the paper and heat is used to permanently fuse the toner to the paper. Laser printers are generally more expensive to purchase than ink-jet printers, although they often print more quickly and are more cost-effective. Lower-end laser printers print only in black and white; however, more expensive printers can produce color copies.

Figure 1.15

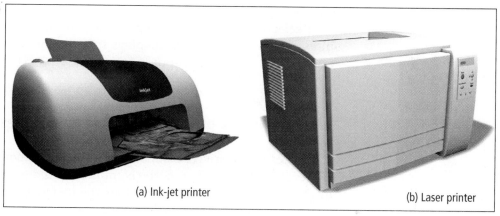

(a) Ink-jet printer

(b) Laser printer

How do you assess a printer's capabilities? When you select a printer, there are some key characteristics to consider. The first of these is print speed, often described as pages per minute (ppm). Print speed can vary depending on the manufacturer and model, and is also affected by whether the page is text-only or if it also includes graphics. Just as with monitors, resolution is also important to print quality. For printing purposes, resolution is expressed as *dots per inch* or *dpi*. The higher the dpi, the better the print quality. Print qualities of 300 to 600 dpi are typical of most printers, although special photo printers can offer resolutions up to 1,200 dpi. Professional printers can reach even higher values. Color output and its related cost is another important consideration. Ink-jet printers offer four- or six-color options. Many ink-jet printers use one cartridge for black ink and another for color. When available, printers that offer a separate cartridge for each color are a practical choice because you only need to replace one color at a time as the cartridges run out. Laser printers use separate toner cartridges for each color.

Speakers and Multimedia Projectors

Are there other output devices? *Speakers* and *multimedia projectors* are also examples of output devices. Many computers include small speakers to allow the user to listen to CDs or DVDs and hear any auditory signals the computer sends. However, if you're serious about multimedia, you will probably want to invest in a better set of speakers for improved performance. Multimedia projectors are used to conduct presentations and training sessions. Imagine how difficult it would be to have a room full of students or conference attendees crowd around a single monitor to view a presentation. A multimedia projector allows information to be projected onto a larger screen so it can easily be viewed by a group.

Multifunction Devices

Some devices, known as **multifunction devices (MFDs)**, combine input and output capabilities. A good example of such a device is the telephone, which allows you to both speak (output) and listen (input) to another person. Other examples include the touchscreen monitor at a convenience store or ATM or the "all-in-one" printer, which combines a printer with a scanner, copier, and fax machine. In each instance, you can use the device to input information by touching the screen to make your selection or by using the device's scanning capability. At the same time, each of these devices displays information on the screen or generates printed copies to output information.

Objective 4
Identify Types of Software and Their Uses

Computer hardware consists of the physical components of the system. However, without software, the computer would just be a collection of mechanical parts. Software provides the instructions that tell the computer what to do. To perform various tasks, the computer requires a set of instructions, called **programs**. These programs enable individuals to use the computer without the need for special programming skills. There are two categories of computer software: system software and application software. Both types of software are required to work effectively with your computer.

System Software

System software provides the instructions that the computer needs to run. It contains the directions needed to start up the computer (known as the **boot process**), checks to ensure everything is in good working order, and enables you to interface with the computer and its peripheral devices so that you can use them. System software consists of two main types of programs: the operating system and utility programs.

Operating Systems

What is the operating system? The **operating system (OS)** is a special computer program that is present on every desktop or notebook computer, in addition to many others ranging from mainframes to PDAs. The operating system controls the way the computer works from the time it is turned on until it is shut down. As shown in Figure 1.16, the operating system manages the various hardware components, including the CPU, memory, storage devices, and peripheral devices. It also coordinates with the various software applications that might be running.

Is it possible to communicate with the operating system? Although the operating system communicates with the computer and its peripherals, it also includes a **user interface** that you can use to interact with the computer. Early operating systems used a DOS-based interface, which required knowledge of special commands that had to be typed accurately to achieve the desired results. As you can imagine, this type of system was not very user-friendly. Most current operating systems use a point-and-click format known as a **graphical user interface (GUI)**. GUIs are more user-friendly and intuitive than DOS systems. Rather than typing specific commands, you can use a mouse to point to and click on an **icon** (a graphical depiction of an object such as a file or program) or a **menu** (a list of commands) to perform a task. GUI operating systems display information on the monitor in the form of rectangular boxes called **screens** or **windows**.

Figure 1.16

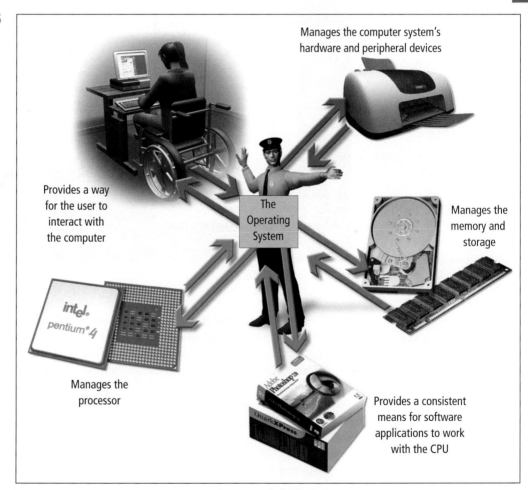

Manages the computer system's hardware and peripheral devices

Provides a way for the user to interact with the computer

The Operating System

Manages the memory and storage

Manages the processor

Provides a consistent means for software applications to work with the CPU

Do all computers need an operating system? The operating system is a critical part of a computer system. Without an OS to provide specific instructions, the computer would be unable to fulfill its four main functions. However, different computers require different types of operating systems. There are several popular operating systems available for home computers. They include Microsoft Windows, Mac OS, and Linux.

Microsoft Windows has the largest market share of the three main operating systems and is found on most of today's desktop and notebook computers. There have been many versions of Microsoft Windows, including Windows 3.0, Windows 95, Windows 98, Windows ME, and Windows Vista. Although a previous version of Windows might be found on an older computer, Windows Vista is the current version installed on most computers. A sample Windows XP desktop is displayed in Figure 1.17.

Figure 1.17

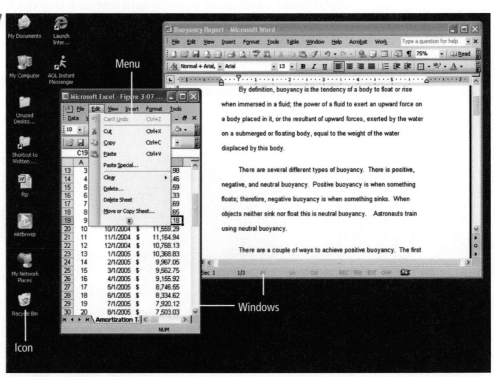

Why are there so many versions of Windows? Software developers are always updating and refining their software to adapt to new technology, respond to vulnerabilities, and improve their product. Because Microsoft also manufactures application software, some of its products have similar names and users can become confused. It's important to note that even though your computer might use Microsoft Windows for its operating system, it may not have Microsoft Office (an application software suite) installed.

Mac OS is an operating system designed specifically for Apple's Macintosh computers. The current version is Mac OS X Tiger. As you can see in Figure 1.18, the Mac OS appears similar to Windows, because it also uses a GUI. In fact, Apple was the first company to introduce a GUI operating system for commercial sale. But, because of the overwhelming popularity of the Windows-based PC, Mac OS has a much smaller market share. There are also significant differences in the way the Mac OS performs. Mac users tend to be very loyal and believe their system is far superior to the Windows system, although there are many Windows users who disagree.

Files

Figure 1.18

Icons

Windows

Icons on the "Dock"
can launch programs

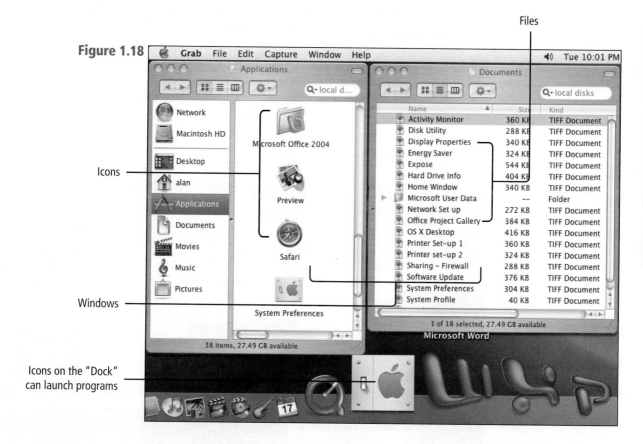

Can Windows run on an Apple computer? Until recently, the Mac OS could not run on a PC, and the Windows OS could not run on a Mac. This was primarily due to the differences in CPUs used by each system. However, now that Apple is also using Intel chips, the concept of a ***dual-boot*** computer (one that can run more than one operating system) running both Mac and Windows operating systems on the same computer has become a reality. Apple has developed Boot Camp, a utility program that will allow Windows XP to be installed on a Mac. While this may appeal to some users—especially those who want to use a Mac but have some applications that will only run on Windows—it is still in the early stages and may not be a good option for everyone.

Linux is an alternative operating system. Based on the UNIX operating system developed for mainframe computers, it also has a dedicated group of users. Linux is an ***open-source*** operating system, which means it is not owned by a single company and some versions are available at no cost.

How is open-source software different from other types of software? Open-source software makes its source code, essentially the program instructions, available to anyone who would like to see it. Programmers are encouraged to work with and change the code as they see fit, in the hope that having many "eyes" looking at the code will streamline and improve it. Proprietary software, such as Microsoft Windows, keeps this code secret and inaccessible to programmers who are not authorized by the software development company.

Why is Linux used? Linux is rarely used by novice computer users, although it is popular among developers and other technologically advanced individuals who prefer to use an alternative operating system.

Some people appreciate the opportunity to work in this more "open" programming environment. However, one of the disadvantages of Linux is that, because no single company is responsible for it, technical support is not easily found. Users might find help from various resources such as user groups and Internet communities. Alternatively, some software companies have chosen to develop and sell a version of Linux that includes a warranty and technical support as a way of alleviating user concerns. Figure 1.19 shows an example of one version of the Linux operating system.

Figure 1.19

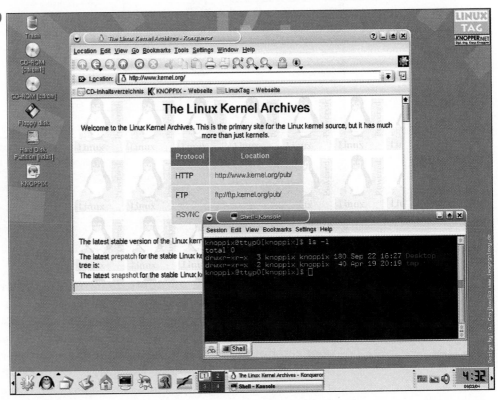

Utility Programs

What are utility programs? Operating system software is the most critical software on the computer, because nothing can run without it. However, **utility programs** are another important component of system software. These small applications handle many important tasks involved with the management and maintenance of your system. Utility programs can be used to help back up important files, remove unwanted files or programs from your system, and schedule various tasks to keep your system running smoothly. Some of these utilities are included with the operating system, whereas others are stand-alone versions that you can purchase or download for free. Figure 1.20 displays a variety of utility programs that ship with the Windows operating system and compares them with similar stand-alone products, describing the function of each utility.

Utility Programs Available within Windows and as Stand-Alone Programs

Windows Utility Program	Off-the-Shelf (Stand-Alone) Utility Program	Function
File Management		
Add/Remove Programs	Aladdin Systems Easy Uninstall	Properly installs/uninstalls software
Windows Explorer File Compression	Win Zip	Reduces file size
Windows System Maintenance and Diagnostics		
Backup	Norton Ghost	Backs up important information
Disk Cleanup	Ontrack System Suite	Removes unnecessary files from hard drive
Disk Defragmenter	Norton SystemWorks	Arranges files on hard drive in sequential order
Error-checking (previously ScanDisk)	Norton CleanSweep	Checks hard drive for unnecessary or damaged files
System Restore	FarStone RestoreIT!	Restores system to a previously established set point
Task Manager		Displays performance measures for processes; provides information on programs and processes running on computer
Task Scheduler		Schedules programs to run automatically at prescribed times

Figure 1.20

Application Software

Although you interact with system software every time you use the computer, in some ways you don't really notice it. *Application software*, on the other hand, is comprised of programs that enable you to accomplish tasks and use the computer in a productive manner.

How do system software and application software work together?
System software is a bit like breathing—you need to do it to live; however, you don't usually think much about it unless something goes wrong. Application software might be compared to a musical instrument like a flute. When a musician combines each of these—her breath and her flute—the result may be a beautiful melody (if she has practiced, of course!). Computer software works together similarly—the system software acts as the "breath," while the application software provides the "instrument," enabling you to create something too.

There are many different kinds of application software, although they often fall into one of several general categories, each of which has a different purpose. These categories include financial and business-related software, graphics and multimedia software, educational and reference software, entertainment software, and communication software. You might be most familiar with productivity software, which includes the following applications:

- **_Word processing software_**—Used to create, edit, format, and save documents and other text-based files. Word processing software enables you to create or edit letters, reports, memos, and many other types of written documents and print them out. Revisions to existing documents can be made quickly and easily, without having to re-create the entire document. Documents created with this type of software can also include graphics, charts, and other graphic elements. Microsoft Word, Lotus Word Pro, and Corel WordPerfect are all examples of word processing programs. A document created using Microsoft Word 2007 is shown in Figure 1.21. Notice that the document contains a graphic element as well as text.

Figure 1.21

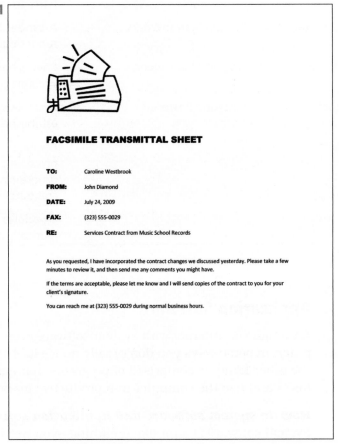

- **_Spreadsheet software_**—Spreadsheet software enables you to perform calculations and other mathematical tasks. Similar to the documents used by accountants, spreadsheets contain data entered in columns and rows and enable you to perform calculations, create scenarios, perform "what-if" analyses, chart and graph data, and format the worksheet layout. A key advantage of spreadsheet software is its capability to recalculate spreadsheets without user intervention. When data used in a calculation or formula is changed, the spreadsheet software automatically updates the worksheet with the correct result. Microsoft Excel, Lotus 1-2-3, and Corel Quattro Pro are examples of spreadsheet programs. Figure 1.22 shows a worksheet created in Microsoft Excel 2007.

Figure 1.22

Store Name	Standard Tires	Performance Tires	Total Standard Sales	Total Performance Sales	Total Tire Sales	Percent of Total Sales
Rio Rancho Auto Gallery						
February Tire Sales						
Diamond Valley	42	38	$ 5,250	$ 8,930	$ 14,180	28.71%
Sierra Vista	26	37	3,250	8,695	11,945	24.19%
Tire Factory	27	26	3,375	6,110	9,485	19.21%
Tread Works	35	40	4,375	9,400	13,775	27.89%
Total	130	141	$ 16,250	$ 33,135	$ 49,385	

Standard Price	$	125
Performance Price	$	235

- **Database software**—Databases are used to store and organize large amounts of data. Typically, database software can be used to manage various types of information, such as that found in large mailing lists, inventories, order histories, and invoicing. Databases help you to enter, store, sort, filter, retrieve, and summarize the information they contain and then generate meaningful reports. Common database programs include Microsoft Access, Lotus Approach, and Corel Paradox. Figure 1.23 shows a database table created in Microsoft Access 2007.

Figure 1.23

Scholarship ID	Scholarship Name	Amount	Sport	Team	Award Date	Student ID
S-01	Southern States Jump Ball Award	$300	Basketball	Men's	09/22/09	STU-1018
S-02	Tech Corridor Sportsmanship Award	$100	Swimming	Men's	05/23/09	STU-1018
S-03	Bay Sports Fellowship Award	$500	Football	Men's	05/01/09	STU-1224
S-04	Golden Sands Country Club Award	$300	Golf	Men's	05/23/09	STU-1231
S-05	Bay Sports Fellowship Award	$500	Basketball	Men's	02/15/09	STU-1264
S-06	Ocean Surf Protection Foundation Award	$750	Swimming	Women's	03/22/09	STU-1510
S-07	Palm Beach Country Club Award	$200	Golf	Women's	06/25/09	STU-1571
S-08	Florida State Baseball Association	$500	Baseball	Men's	01/16/09	STU-1581
S-09	Florida State Baseball Association	$300	Baseball	Men's	10/30/09	STU-1018
S-10	Ocean Bay Volleyball Club Leadership Award	$200	Tennis	Women's	05/06/09	STU-1510
S-11	June Claudino Walters Memorial Award	$200	Volleyball	Women's	11/04/09	STU-1715
S-12	Florida Sportswomen Foundation Award	$300	Basketball	Women's	05/06/09	STU-1111
S-13	Home Run Foundation Award	$200	Baseball	Men's	08/04/09	STU-1888
S-14	Florida Port Science Achievement Award	$750	Football	Men's	11/12/09	STU-1810
S-15	Roundball Academic Achievement Award	$500	Basketball	Men's	01/25/09	STU-1859
S-16	Florida Port Country Club Foundation Award	$400	Swimming	Women's	05/23/09	STU-1868
S-17	Go To The Net Award	$200	Tennis	Men's	07/29/09	STU-1888
S-18	Pinellas Academic Achievement Award	$250	Volleyball	Women's	05/21/09	STU-1125
S-19	Florida Port Country Club Foundation Award	$200	Golf	Men's	12/06/09	STU-1167
S-20	Lee Henry Foundation Award	$400	Tennis	Women's	04/14/09	STU-1111
S-21	Silver Helmet Award	$100	Football	Men's	07/12/09	STU-1921
S-22	Spike It Award	$200	Volleyball	Women's	02/02/09	STU-1977
S-23	Bay Town Sports Award	$500	Basketball	Men's	09/15/09	STU-1112
S-24	Bay Sports Fellowship Award	$500	Basketball	Women's	04/10/09	STU-1990
S-25	Hoops National Winner Award	$400	Basketball	Women's	12/22/09	STU-1125

- **Presentation software**—Because of presentation software, lecturers no longer need to rely on flip charts, slide projectors, or overhead transparencies for their presentations. This software is used to create graphic presentations, known as slide shows, that can be shown to large groups by means of an overhead projector or displayed on the Web. Presentation software is also used to create audience handouts, speaker notes, and other materials that can be used during an oral presentation or for distribution to an audience. Microsoft PowerPoint, Lotus Freelance Graphics, and Corel Presentations are examples of presentation software programs. Figure 1.24 shows a presentation created with Microsoft PowerPoint 2007.

Figure 1.24

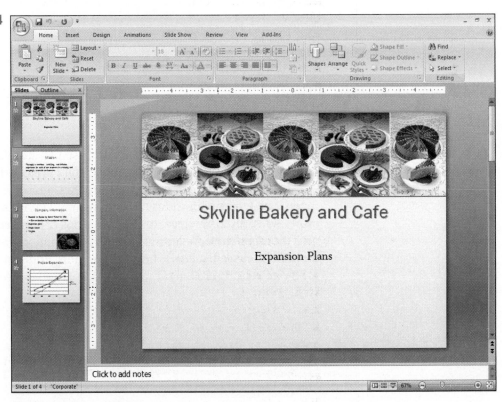

- **Communication and organizational software**—Communication software can cover a broad range of tasks including videoconferencing and telephony. However, applications within the productivity category are most often used to send and receive e-mail. These applications typically include an address book, a calendar, and task functions, which help users organize their personal and professional responsibilities. Microsoft Outlook, Lotus Notes, and Corel WordPerfect Mail are examples of communication and organizational software. Figure 1.25 shows an example of a calendar in Microsoft Outlook 2007.

Figure 1.25

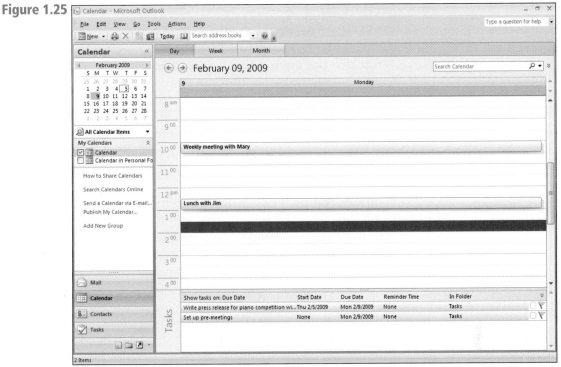

What is a software suite? Although it is possible to buy any of the previous applications separately, most software manufacturers, including Microsoft, Corel, and Lotus, also group applications together into a package called a *suite*. This can be an economical way to purchase software if you need some or all of the programs in the suite. The cost of a suite is usually less than the total cost of purchasing each of the applications individually. Additionally, because products from the same company have many common elements, such as basic window design and layout, toolbars containing similar tools, dictionaries, and media galleries, many users find this familiarity makes it easier to switch between the programs in a suite. Examples of suites include Microsoft Office, Corel WordPerfect Office, and Lotus SmartSuite.

What are some other common software applications? As mentioned earlier, there are many different types of application software besides productivity software, each one with a specific function. You might use Microsoft Publisher or QuarkXPress to create a newsletter or brochure. Bookkeepers rely on special accounting packages such as Peachtree Accounting or QuickBooks to balance the books and handle other accounting functions. Graphic designers turn to packages like Adobe Photoshop or Adobe Illustrator to develop creative artwork. You might use Microsoft FrontPage or Macromedia Dreamweaver to create your own Web site. To identify other software programs and their uses, visit a home electronics or discount store to see which programs they stock, or browse the shelves of your local bookstore for some of the latest "how-to" information.

Objective 5
Describe Networks and Define Network Terms

What are the components of a network? Recall that computers and the various peripherals that are connected to them are called hardware. However, connecting one computer to another creates a ***network***. Networks consist of two or more connected computers plus the various peripheral devices that are attached to them. Each object connected to a network, whether it is a computer or a peripheral device, is known as a ***node***.

Why are computers connected to networks? Some of the benefits of computer networks include the ability to share software applications and resources such as printers and scanners. Improved communication and data sharing are additional benefits. Computers can be connected to a network in several ways. They can use existing telephone wires or power lines, or use coaxial, unshielded twisted pair (UTP), or fiber-optic cable. Networks can also be ***wireless***, in which case they use radio waves instead of wires or cables to connect.

Can networks be different sizes? A computer network that connects computers reasonably close together, such as within a home or in a small office or business, is called a ***local area network (LAN).*** Usually these networks are contained within a single building or group of adjacent buildings. If the network begins to cover a larger geographic area or begins to include other networks, it becomes a ***wide area network (WAN).*** An example of this is the network used by Penn State University. Penn State has many campuses located across the state of Pennsylvania. Because the different campuses are connected through a WAN, students and teachers are able to use a computer in one location and access files or resources located at any of the other campuses, wherever they might be located. Both LANs and WANs can be wired or wireless. Wired LANs might use phone lines or cable connections, while wired WANs might use phone lines, satellites, or special leased lines, known as T-1 or T-3 lines, for high-speed communication. In fact, the Internet is actually the largest network of all because it connects computers around the world.

How are networks configured? Networks can be configured in several ways. There are two main categories: peer-to-peer and client/server. ***Peer-to-peer*** or ***P2P networks*** are most commonly found in homes and small businesses. In a peer-to-peer network, each node on the network can communicate with every other node. Peer-to-peer networks are relatively easy to set up, but tend to be rather small. This makes them ideal for home use, although not as desirable in the workplace. If a network has more than ten nodes, it is generally best to use the ***client/server network*** instead. Remember that a node can be a computer, printer, scanner, modem, or any other peripheral device that can be connected to a computer. Therefore, it isn't difficult to find more than ten nodes in an office or business setting.

How is a client/server network different from a P2P network?
Client/server networks typically have two different types of computers.

The **client** is the computer used at your desk or workstation to write letters, send e-mail, produce invoices, or perform any of the many tasks that can be accomplished with a computer. The client computer is the one most people directly interact with. In contrast, the **server** computer is typically kept in a secure location and is used to manage network resources. If a server is assigned to handle only specific tasks, it is known as a **dedicated server.** For instance, a Web server is used to deliver Web pages, a file server is used to store and archive files, and a print server manages the printing resources for the network. Each of these is a dedicated server.

Network topology describes the different types of network architecture used for client/server networks. Just as there are different sizes and styles of buildings that are designed for different purposes, networks are designed to be physically configured and connected in different ways.

Which topologies are used most often? The three most common layouts are explained in the following list:

- **Bus topology** connects each node to a single, central high-speed line known as a bus. No server is used, and although it is possible for each node to communicate with all the others, they can only do so one at a time. If one computer or device is sending over the network, all the others must wait until the transmission is complete before they can begin. Because this is an inexpensive and easy way to connect, this topology is often found in peer-to-peer networks.

- **Ring topology**, sometimes known as **token-ring topology**, connects each node to the next, forming a loop or a circle. The data that's sent is passed from node to node, traveling around the circle in only one direction. A token travels around the ring until one of the nodes is ready to send a transmission. The node then holds the token until the transmission is finished, preventing any of the other devices from sending until the token is released to make its way around the circle again. This type of topology gives each device an equal chance of being able to send data and prevents one node from doing all the communicating.

- **Star topology** is the most frequent networking style used for businesses. It offers a high degree of flexibility. Each node is connected to a special device known as a switch, which is centrally located. Each node must go through the switch to communicate with the others. If something happens to one node, the others are still able to communicate.

Figure 1.26 shows an example of each of these layouts, and Figure 1.27 discusses the advantages and disadvantages of each of these topographies.

Figure 1.26

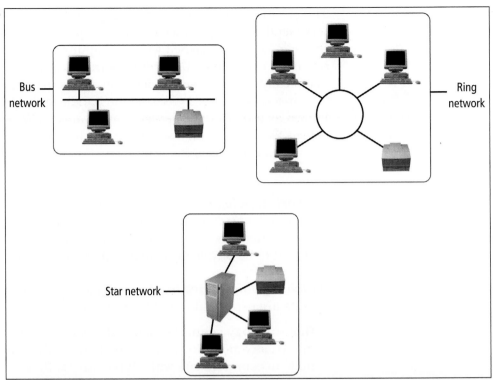

Bus network

Ring network

Star network

Advantages and Disadvantages of Bus, Ring, and Star Topologies

Topology	Advantages	Disadvantages
Bus	Uses a minimal amount of cabling. Easy, reliable, and inexpensive to install.	Breaks in the cable can disable the network. Large numbers of users will greatly decrease performance because of high volumes of data traffic.
Ring	Allocates access to the network fairly. Performance remains acceptable even with large numbers of users.	Adding or removing nodes disables the network. Failure of one computer can bring down the entire network. Problems in data transmission can sometimes be difficult to find.
Star	Failure of one computer does not affect other computers on the network. Centralized design simplifies trouble-shooting and repairs. Easy to add additional computers or network segments as needed (high scalability). Performance remains acceptable even with large numbers of users.	Requires more cable and is often more expensive than a bus or ring topology. The switch is a central point of failure. If it fails, all computers connected to that switch are affected.

Figure 1.27

38 **Computer Concepts** | Chapter 1: Basic Computer Concepts

Objective 6
Identify Safe Computing Practices

Being computer fluent implies you are a responsible computer user. This means more than just understanding the key components of a computer or the differences between hardware and software. Responsible computer users also know how to properly maintain their computers, back up necessary data, and protect themselves and others from security breaches and attacks.

Computer Maintenance

The first step to protect your computer and the valuable information it contains is to establish a regular maintenance routine. Backup utility programs, which may be part of your system software or purchased separately, enable you to back up your files. You can back up everything on your computer, just one or two important files, or anything in between. People often think that the computer is the most expensive item to replace if their hard drive fails. In reality, it is usually all the lost information that was contained on the hard drive that is the most costly to replace, if it is even possible to do so. Think about the types of files you might have on your own computer—financial records, resumes, homework or school projects, your CD collection and purchased music files, and family photos—then imagine how you would re-create these files if they were irretrievably damaged. Would you be able to find them again? If you back up files on a regular basis and store the backups in a secure location, you lessen the impact that a mechanical failure or security breach will have on your data.

What other types of maintenance tasks should be performed? In addition to backing up files, regular file maintenance also helps to maintain order in your system. Several useful Windows utilities can be accessed from the System Tools folder. You can access the System Tools folder by clicking Start, clicking All Programs, and then clicking Accessories. Disk Cleanup scans the hard drive and removes unnecessary files such as those found in the Recycle Bin, in addition to temporary Internet files and other temporary files created by various programs. It is possible to adjust the settings and select which files to delete and which files to retain.

Similarly, the Disk Defragmenter scans the hard drive. However, rather than removing files, it attempts to reallocate files so they use the available hard drive space more efficiently. Recall that data is stored on hard drives in sectors and tracks. As file sizes change, they can outgrow their original location. When that happens, the remaining portion of the file may be stored elsewhere. If a file size decreases, or a file is deleted, this can create a blank area on the hard drive. Defragmenting a hard drive enables scattered portions of files to be regrouped and open spaces to be rearranged. This results in faster and more efficient file access, which improves the response time of the hard drive.

Is there a way to automate these maintenance tasks? Running these programs can be time consuming, especially when you want to use your computer for other tasks. It is also easy to forget to do these things on a regular basis. That is why newer versions of Windows include a Scheduled Task Wizard. This utility, listed as Scheduled Tasks in the System Tools folder, enables you to select the best time for each task to run, in addition to how often, which makes the whole process automatic. Figure 1.28 shows the Scheduled Task Wizard being used to set up the Disk Cleanup task.

Figure 1.28

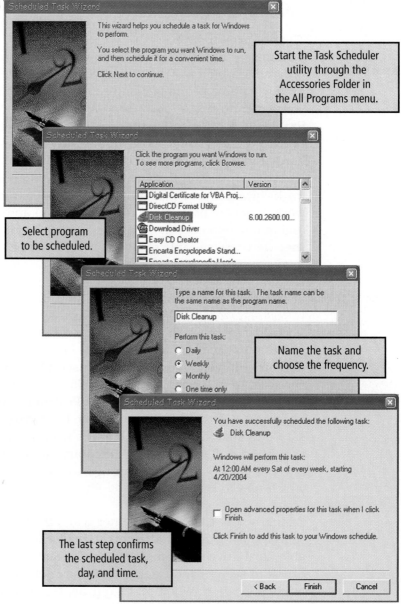

Start the Task Scheduler utility through the Accessories Folder in the All Programs menu.

Select program to be scheduled.

Name the task and choose the frequency.

The last step confirms the scheduled task, day, and time.

Can changes to my system be undone? Sometimes when new software is installed on a computer, the results are not what you anticipated. Instead of playing a new game, you find your system stops responding each time you start it. Or, you might find the new driver you installed for your printer is causing conflicts. Even though you've tried to uninstall the software, the system is still not right.

Fortunately, if you are running a newer version of Windows the System Restore utility (also found in the System Tools folder) can come to the rescue. Periodically, Windows creates a **restore point**, which records all the settings for your system. It's similar to taking a picture of how everything is currently set up. See System Restore in action in Figure 1.29.

It is also possible to set manual restore points, and it is highly recommended that you set one before installing new software or hardware, or when making any major changes to your system. If you experience a problem with your system after the new software is installed, you can roll your system back to an earlier restore point when the system was working correctly. Think of it as an Undo button for your operating system. The good news is, returning to an earlier restore point affects only your system settings—it does not delete any of the data files you may have created during the interval.

Figure 1.29

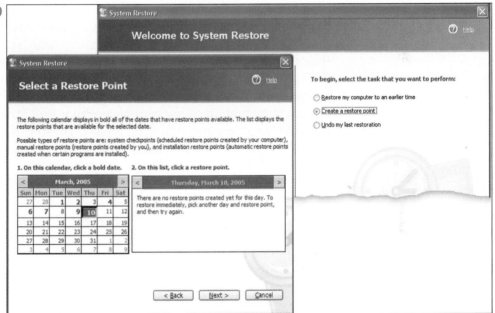

Viruses

Establishing the habit of performing regular maintenance on your computer is one way to protect it, and yourself, from data loss. But there are many other dangers you need to be aware of too. Viruses, spyware, and hackers are all out there waiting to pounce on the unwary computer user.

What are viruses and how do they get on the computer? Computer ***viruses*** are malicious codes or programs that are usually installed on your computer without your knowledge and against your wishes. The severity of a virus can vary. Some viruses merely seem to be nuisances or might not even be obvious to the user; some cause files to be corrupted or erased; and others are capable of shutting down a computer and erasing the entire hard drive. Viruses infect a system and then attach themselves to a program or file to spread to other users.

Viruses can be distributed in several ways. In the early days of computers, viruses were spread by sharing infected floppy disks. Now, due to the ease in which files can be shared over the Internet, viruses are able to spread much more quickly. One of the most common ways to send a virus is through e-mail attachments. Security experts recommend that you never open an e-mail attachment unless you have first scanned it with antivirus software to determine that it is virus-free. Experts also recommend that unless you know the sender and have been expecting the e-mail attachment, it is best to delete the attachment without ever opening it. File-sharing services are another source for these types of problems.

Are viruses and worms the same thing? **Worms** are similar to viruses because they are also malicious programs that spread from computer to computer; however, unlike viruses, worms are able to do this without any human interaction and are able to replicate themselves so numerous copies can be sent. Worms can burrow into your e-mail address book, or locate e-mail addresses on files saved on your hard drive, then send themselves out without any help from you. When it reaches the e-mail recipient, it does the same thing to the recipient's Address Book. Also, because worms can quickly replicate themselves, they can repeat this scenario over and over. Just the sheer amount of traffic they cause on a network can be enough to bring an entire company to a grinding halt. Worms can also open a "back door" to your system, which enables hackers access to it and gives them the ability to control your computer remotely. Sasser, Blaster, NetSky, and MyDoom are all worms that have created a great deal of trouble in recent years.

Trojan horses are not truly viruses because they do not duplicate themselves or infect other files; however, they can be just as problematic. At first glance, a Trojan horse often appears to be a desirable software program. Perhaps it is a free screensaver program or a set of animated cursors. Unfortunately, these programs come with an unwanted and hidden agenda. After the software is installed, the effects can be similar to those that viruses or worms cause. Before you install new software, it is important to scan the program files with antivirus software to ensure there are no Trojan horses lurking there. And, as with unknown e-mail attachments, it is important to be skeptical about free software—it's not often that you really get something for nothing!

Spyware

How is spyware different from viruses? **Spyware** is software designed to capture personal and confidential information that resides on your system and send it elsewhere. It has quickly become as large a problem as viruses. Spyware's primary threat is to your privacy and confidentiality. Although spyware is not usually intended to harm your system, it can sometimes have that effect on it. **Adware** is spyware that tracks your Internet browsing and can install malicious cookies on your computer. A **cookie** is a small text file that contains information that can identify you to a Web site. Cookies are not necessarily bad. They are useful when they are used to help personalize your Web browsing experience, but cookies can threaten your privacy if they are used to reveal too much information.

How can you tell if spyware is on a computer? One symptom that indicates adware is on a computer is an increase in the number of pop-up ads the user receives, some of which might even address the user by name! Adware can generate pop-up ads even when you're not online. Some types of adware can also reset a Web browser's home page to a page of its choosing and take control of the search engine, directing you to Web sites that have been predetermined by the adware.

Are there other privacy threats? **Key loggers** are another type of spyware. In this case, a software program records every keystroke made on the computer. Key loggers can capture all sorts of confidential information this way—passwords, credit card numbers, bank account numbers, and so on—and then relay this information elsewhere. Entire e-mail messages and instant messaging conversations can be recorded this way too. Some key loggers are hardware, rather than software, although they perform the same devious function. Such hardware devices can be attached between the keyboard and the computer. The information stolen through the use of key loggers can easily make you a victim of identity theft. Trojan horses can be used to distribute key loggers and other types of spyware just as easily as they deliver viruses.

How can you avoid being a victim? To minimize the risk of having spyware installed on your computer, there are some practical precautions you can take. One of the most prevalent methods of spreading spyware is through file-sharing services, such as Morpheus or Kazaa. Not only can the file-sharing software include spyware, but often the files you think you are downloading for free are infected too. Although it's tempting to get the newest song or video for free from such a site, don't risk it!

This problem can be avoided if you use one of the legitimate, pay-as-you-go file-sharing services such as iTunes or the reincarnated Napster. Additionally, be cautious when you download and install freeware or shareware software. Make sure you deal with a reputable software publisher, scan the downloaded software for viruses and spyware, and read the licensing agreement. Some licensing agreements actually include information about additional software that will be automatically installed if you accept it.

Another way to prevent spyware is to avoid pop-up and banner ads whenever possible. You should never click on them. Often the "No Thanks" button is just a ruse to get you to click it and enable the spyware installation. Close pop-up ads by clicking the Close button in the top right corner. Even better, installing pop-up blocking software can help to eliminate this risk almost entirely.

If you are running the most recent version of Windows you already have a pop-up blocker available to you. You can view the pop-up blocker settings for Windows XP in Figure 1.30 and access this dialog box through Internet Explorer's Tools menu. Many popular search engines, such as Google and Yahoo!, also include pop-up blocking features in their toolbars, which you can download at no charge. It is also wise to avoid questionable Web sites, because some of them can install spyware on your system just by visiting the site.

Figure 1.30

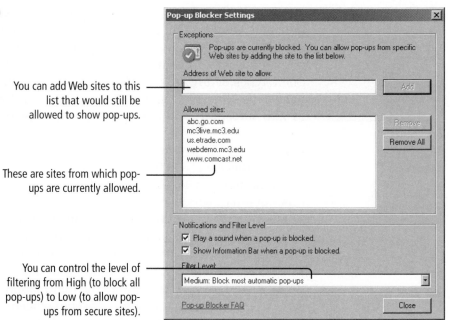

You can add Web sites to this list that would still be allowed to show pop-ups.

These are sites from which pop-ups are currently allowed.

You can control the level of filtering from High (to block all pop-ups) to Low (to allow pop-ups from secure sites).

Protecting Yourself and Your Computer

In addition to being cautious in your Internet travels, there are some proactive measures you can take to protect yourself and your computer from viruses and spyware. These include

- **Software updates and patches**—Keeping your operating system and software up-to-date is critical. Software manufacturers are constantly on the lookout for security threats, and they issue updates and patches to help protect your system. Check for these and install them regularly. Software manufacturers have begun to implement automated procedures to check and install such updates. If your computer has this capability, it's a good idea to use this feature. Figure 1.31 shows the Windows XP System Properties dialog box, with the Automatic Updates tab open.

Figure 1.31

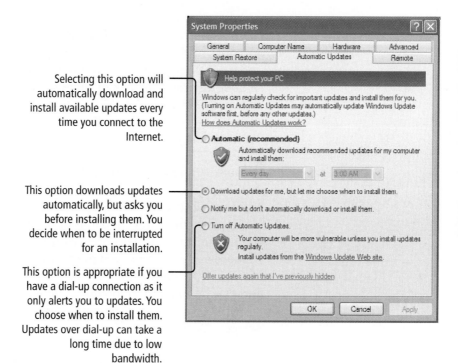

Selecting this option will automatically download and install available updates every time you connect to the Internet.

This option downloads updates automatically, but asks you before installing them. You decide when to be interrupted for an installation.

This option is appropriate if you have a dial-up connection as it only alerts you to updates. You choose when to install them. Updates over dial-up can take a long time due to low bandwidth.

- *Antivirus and antispyware software—Antivirus software* is a utility program used to search your hard drive and files for viruses, and remove those that are found. *Antispyware software* works in a similar fashion, but searches for spyware rather than viruses. No computer should be without this protection. Many users erroneously think that because they aren't regularly online or use only a slow dial-up connection, they aren't a target. Nothing could be further from the truth! Recent studies show more than two-thirds of all computer users have some form of virus or spyware on their system.

  There are a variety of antivirus and antispyware products available. Unfortunately, there are also a lot of dishonest companies purporting to offer these products. Too often, these are really scams that will actually install spyware or viruses on your system! To avoid being scammed or downloading something malicious, you should never respond to offers that are received in a pop-up ad or unsolicited e-mail. To obtain legitimate products, it is best to purchase them from the manufacturer's Web site or from a local retailer. Additionally, some Internet Service Providers are beginning to provide some of these products as part of their services.

  Some well-known antivirus products include Norton AntiVirus (*www.symantec.com*), McAfee VirusScan (*www.mcafee.com*), and AVG Anti-Virus (*www.grisoft.com*). Antispyware products include eTrust PestPatrol (*www.pestpatrol.com*), Ad-Aware (*www.lavasoft.com*), and Spybot Search & Destroy (*www.safer-networking.org*). You can search for other products at popular download sites such as Download.com (*www.download.com*) or Tucows (*www.tucows.com*) but you should be sure to read the software reviews and evaluate their usefulness before downloading or installing them.

  It is best to use only one antivirus product, because running more than one can cause conflicts between the programs. However, because there are so many different types of spyware, antispyware products may address these problems in different ways. Experts recommend running at least two different antispyware applications in order to catch as many spyware programs as possible. It's not enough to install antivirus and antispyware software on your system; you need to update it frequently—at least once a week. Doing so will protect you against any new viruses or spyware created since the last time you checked. Software should be set to scan incoming data—files, e-mail, and so on—but regular full-system scans should be conducted on a weekly basis as well.

- **Personal firewalls**—Firewalls may be software programs or hardware devices, although their purpose is the same—to prevent unauthorized access to your computer. When a firewall is installed properly, it can make your computer invisible to hackers and other invaders. Not only can a good firewall help prevent infections and identity theft; it can also prevent hackers from accessing your computer and turning it into a **zombie**. A zombie computer is one that can be controlled remotely and can be used to help spread viruses, spyware, or junk e-mail known as **spam**. Zombie computers can also be used in **denial of service (DoS)** attacks. DoS attacks occur when a large number of computers try to access a Web site at the same time, effectively overloading it and causing it to shut down. If you are using Windows XP or Windows Vista you already have a firewall available to you.

Figure 1.32 shows the Windows XP Firewall dialog box. You can access the firewall settings by clicking Start, and then clicking Control Panel and clicking Windows Security Center. Click Windows Firewall from the Security Center. Note that you can also access Windows Update from this area too.

Figure 1.32

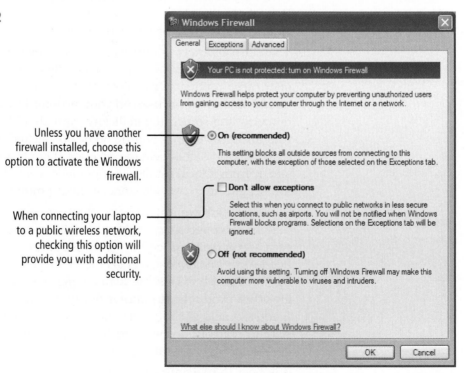

Unless you have another firewall installed, choose this option to activate the Windows firewall.

When connecting your laptop to a public wireless network, checking this option will provide you with additional security.

What else should I look out for? It might sound simple, but when online, do not give out personal information unless it is for legitimate purposes. It is important to avoid spam e-mail and ***phishing*** attacks— e-mails that masquerade as authentic entities such as banks and credit card companies and ask for confidential information. Legitimate organizations will not ask for passwords, bank account numbers, or credit card details through e-mail. It is also possible to check for hoaxes and scams at a variety of Web sites, including many of the antivirus and antispyware sites. When in doubt, do some research to see if the request you've received is legitimate. If necessary, make a telephone call to the agency in question. Viewing such requests with a critical eye can help you avoid online scams and hoaxes.

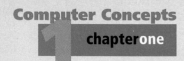

Computer Concepts

1 chapterone

Summary

In this chapter, you examined the benefits of computer fluency and identified the four basic functions of computing. You explored the various types of computers and their components, including CPUs, RAM, and storage devices. This chapter also discussed how to evaluate a computer system and understand the terminology used to measure storage capacity, memory, and microprocessor speed. Various hardware and peripheral devices were reviewed, including input and output devices, and different types of storage media. You explored the basic types of computer software—system software and application software—and the different uses for each type. You identified various types of networks and the different ways networks can be configured. You also reviewed ways to maintain your computer and keep it safe from various threats, including viruses and spyware.

Key Terms

Content-Based Assessments

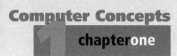
Key Terms

Content-Based Assessments

Key Terms

Computer Concepts

chapterone

Matching

Match each term in the second column with its correct definition in the first column. Write the letter of the term on the blank line in front of the correct definition.

____ **1.** Computer programs.

____ **2.** Programs that enable you to accomplish tasks and use the computer in a productive manner.

____ **3.** Two or more computers connected together to enable resource sharing.

____ **4.** Used to manage network resources, this type of computer can be dedicated to a specific task.

____ **5.** Floppy disks use this type of storage media.

____ **6.** The layout or design/arrangement of computers connected to a network.

____ **7.** A peripheral device uses this to attach to the computer.

____ **8.** An electronic system that contains input, processing, output, and storage units.

____ **9.** The physical components of a computer system.

____ **10.** Hardware connected outside the main computer system unit.

____ **11.** The hardware unit that contains the CPU, memory, hard disk, and power supply.

____ **12.** The unit that contains the circuitry that enables a computer system to operate.

____ **13.** The temporary storage available inside the computer.

____ **14.** The processing unit.

____ **15.** This type of program threatens a user's privacy.

A Application software

B Computer

C Computer network

D Console/system unit

E CPU

F Hardware

G Magnetic

H Memory (RAM)

I Motherboard/system board

J Peripherals

K Port

L Server

M Software

N Spyware

O Topology

Fill in the Blank

Write the correct word in the space provided.

1. Used to perform complex, dedicated tasks, the _____ is the fastest and most expensive computer.

2. The four basic functions of a computer are _____, _____, _____, and _____.

3. Someone with the basic skills and knowledge of a responsible computer user is considered to be computer _____.

4. Personal digital assistants (PDAs) are also known as _____ computers.

5. _____ is data that has been processed and presented in an organized format.

6. The control unit and the arithmetic logic unit are located in the _____.

7. _____ measures how quickly the CPU processes data.

8. An object connected to a network is known as a(n) _____.

9. A(n) _____ network is often found in homes and allows each node to communicate with all the others.

10. A(n) _____ records system settings and can be used to roll back a system to an earlier date in case a software installation has unexpected results.

11. When information is displayed on a monitor it is known as _____ copy.

12. The number of pixels displayed on the screen determines a monitor's _____.

13. _____ printers use a drum and toner in the printing process.

14. The quality of a printed page is measured in dpi, which is an acronym for _____.

15. The point-and-click format that modern operating systems use is called a(n) _____.

Content-Based Assessments

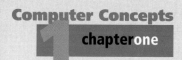
Multiple Choice

Circle the letter of the item that correctly answers the question.

1. Which of the following requires one byte of storage?

   a. Page

   b. Paragraph

   c. Sentence

   d. Character

2. Which of the following terms represents the fastest CPU speed?

   a. 733 MHz

   b. 286 MHz

   c. 2 GHz

   d. 2 GB

3. Which of the following is not an input device?

   a. Keyboard

   b. Speaker

   c. Mouse

   d. Stylus

4. Which of the following is an example of optical storage?

   a. Disk drive

   b. Flash card

   c. Memory

   d. Compact disc

5. Which of the following is not a type of computer?

   a. Mainframe

   b. Multitask

   c. Server

   d. Supercomputer

6. Before a computer can process data, where must data be stored?

   a. On a disk

   b. In computer memory

   c. In the control unit

   d. On the monitor

Content-Based Assessments

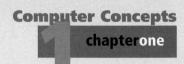
Multiple Choice

7. What term, related to computers, means billions?

   a. Byte

   b. Mega

   c. Giga

   d. Hertz

8. Which of the following is not a type of microcomputer?

   a. Desktop

   b. Notebook

   c. Personal digital assistant

   d. Microprocessor

9. Which of the following can make a computer invisible to hackers?

   a. Disk defragmenter

   b. Antivirus software

   c. Firewall

   d. Key logger

10. Which of the following is capable of opening a "back door" on a computer and is able to spread without human interaction?

   a. Trojan horse

   b. Worm

   c. Adware

   d. Zombie

Glossary

Adware Spyware that tracks a user's Internet browsing and installs malicious cookies.

Antispyware software A program that protects a computer from malicious software designed to threaten privacy and confidentiality.

Antivirus software A program that protects a computer from malicious codes such as viruses, worms, and Trojan horses.

Application software Programs with which you accomplish tasks such as word processing, photo editing, or sending e-mail, and use the computer in a productive manner.

Arithmetic logic unit (ALU) Part of the CPU that performs all the arithmetic and logic functions for the computer; handles addition, subtraction, multiplication, and division, and also makes logical and comparison decisions.

Arrow keys The arrow keys found at the bottom center section of the keyboard, used to move the insertion point within the program window.

Audio port A port that connects audio equipment to the sound card of a computer to facilitate the exchange of data.

Backup tape drive A storage device used to save data to tapes resembling audiocassettes.

Bluetooth Wireless technology that uses radio waves to transmit data over short distances, and often used with mobile devices.

Boot The process of starting up a computer.

Boot process See Boot.

Burn The process of recording data to optical media such as a CD or DVD.

Bus topology A networking configuration in which all devices are connected to a central high-speed cable called the bus or backbone.

Cathode-ray tube (CRT) A picture tube device used in a monitor, similar to a television.

CD burner An optical storage device capable of reading data from and writing data to a CD.

CD drive A storage device used to read and, possibly, write data to CD.

Central processing unit (CPU) The part of the computer responsible for controlling all the commands and tasks the computer performs, acting as the brain of the computer.

Click To press the left (or primary) mouse button once.

Client In a client/server network, this is the computer most people interact with to request information from the server and to perform many of the tasks that can be accomplished with a computer.

Client/server network A network consisting of client and server computers; often used in businesses.

Clock speed A measurement of how quickly a CPU processes data, an indication of a CPU's processing power.

Communication or organizational software A program such as Microsoft Outlook, used to send and retrieve e-mail and manage day-to-day tasks.

Computer A programmable electronic device that can input, process, output, and store data.

Computer fluent The term used to describe a person who understands the capabilities and limitations of computers and knows how to use computer technology to accomplish tasks.

Connectivity port A port that enables a computer to be connected to other devices or systems, such as networks, modems, and the Internet.

Control keys Special keys, such as Ctrl, Alt, or Esc, used to increase keyboard functionality or provide shortcuts.

Control unit The part of the CPU responsible for obtaining instructions from the computer's memory; the control unit interprets the instructions and executes them, thereby coordinating the activities of all the other computer components.

Cookie A small text file containing information that identifies a visitor to a Web site.

CPU See Central processing unit.

CRT See Cathode-ray tube.

Data Words, numbers, sounds, or pictures that represent facts about people, events, things, or ideas.

Database software Programs, such as Microsoft Access, used to store and organize large amounts of data and perform complex tasks such as sorting and querying to generate specialized reports.

Dedicated server A computer that is assigned to handle one specific task on a network.

Denial of service (DoS) An attack caused when a large number of computers attempt to access a Web site at the same time, effectively overloading it and causing it to shut down.

Desktop computer A class of microcomputer, such as a PC or a Mac.

Digital camera A type of camera that saves photographs in a digital format rather than on film.

Digital Video Interface (DVI) port A port used to connect an LCD monitor to a computer in order to use a pure digital signal.

Digital video recorder A device used to record video in digital format directly to a hard drive, without the need for videotape.

Display screen See Monitor.

Dot matrix An impact printer, useful for printing multi-page forms.

Dot pitch The diagonal distance between adjacent pixels, measured in millimeters and that is used to determine image quality for monitors.

Dots per inch (dpi) A measurement of printer resolution.

Double-click The action of clicking the left mouse button twice in rapid succession while keeping the mouse still.

Drag The action of moving something from one location on the screen to another; the action of dragging includes releasing the mouse button at the desired time or location.

Dual-boot A system with two different operating systems installed, giving the user the option to boot the computer using either one.

Dual-core A CPU that includes two microprocessors on a single integrated circuit. See also Multicore.

DVD drive A storage device used to read and, possibly, write data to DVD.

DVI port See Digital Video Interface (DVI) port.

Embedded computers Components of larger products, devices that perform pre-defined tasks using specially programmed processors.

Ethernet port A port, slightly larger than a telephone jack, that can transmit data at speeds up to 1,000 megabits per second (Mbps) and is usually used to connect to a cable modem or a network.

Firewall See Personal firewall.

FireWire port A port used to send data at rates up to 800 megabits per second (Mbps), frequently used for digital cameras or digital video recorders.

Flash drive A small, portable, digital storage device that connects to a computer's USB port; also called a thumb drive, jump drive, or USB drive.

Flash memory Portable, nonvolatile memory, that uses electronic, solid-state circuitry.

Flat panel See Liquid crystal display.

Flat screen A type of screen used in CRT monitors, and which differs from flat panel monitors.

Floppy disk drive (or floppy drive) The original storage device for a microcomputer, which enables portable, permanent storage on floppy disks.

Function key The keys, numbered F1 through F12, located above the numeric keys on a keyboard that have different functions depending upon the software program in use.

Gigabyte (GB) Approximately one billion bytes; a unit of measure for memory and storage space.

Gigahertz (GHz) One billion hertz; hertz is the unit of measure for processor speed.

Graphical user interface (GUI) A computer interface with which you interact with the computer through the use of graphics and point-and-click technology; GUIs show documents as they will look in their final form.

GUI See Graphical user interface.

Handheld computers See Personal digital assistant.

Hard copy Data or information retrieved from a computer and printed.

Hard disk drive (or hard drive) Permanent storage device, located within the system unit, that holds all permanently stored software and data.

Hardware The physical components of the computer and any equipment connected to it.

Hyperthreading Technology that allows a CPU to emulate multiple processors, improving processing power and speed.

Icon A graphic representation of an object that you can click to open that object.

Impact A type of printer that resembles a typewriter; a key and ink ribbon are used to imprint a character on paper.

Information Data that has been organized in a useful manner.

Information processing cycle The cycle composed of the four basic computer functions: input, process, output, and storage.

Ink-jet Type of printer that uses a special nozzle and ink cartridges to distribute liquid ink on the surface of the paper.

Input The act of entering data into a computer.

Input devices Computer hardware used to enter data and instructions into a computer; examples include the keyboard, mouse, stylus, scanner, microphone, and digital camera.

Internet control key Usually found at the top of a keyboard, this type of key can be used for various Internet-related activities including opening a Web browser and sending e-mail.

IrDA port A port enabling data transmission through the use of infrared light waves; the devices sharing data require a clear line of site with no visual obstructions.

Joysticks Input devices used to control actions and movement within computer games.

Key logger A software program or hardware device that records every keystroke made on the computer.

Keyboard The hardware device used to input typed data and commands into a computer.

LAN See Local area network.

Laser A type of printer that uses a drum, static electricity, and a laser to distribute dry ink or toner on the surface of the paper.

LCD See Liquid crystal display.

Linux An open-source operating system based on the UNIX operating system developed for mainframe computers.

Liquid crystal display (LCD) Technology used in flat panel monitors, resulting in thinner and lighter monitors.

Local area network (LAN) A network in which the nodes are located within a small geographic area.

Mac OS The operating system designed specifically for Apple's Mac computers.

Magnetic A type of storage process using magnetized film to store data; used by media such as floppy disks or Zip disks.

Mainframe A large computer capable of performing more than one task at the same time and supporting many users simultaneously.

Megabyte (MB) Approximately one million bytes; a unit of measure for memory and storage space.

Megahertz (MHz) One million hertz; hertz is the unit of measure for processor speed.

Menu A list of commands within a category.

MFD See Multifunction device.

Microcomputer The computer most users are familiar with, ranging in size from large desktop systems to handheld devices.

Microphones Input devices used to digitally record sound.

Microprocessor chip See Central processing unit.

Microsoft Windows The operating system found on most microcomputers.

MIDI port Musical Instrument Digital Interface port used to connect electronic musical instruments to a system.

Mobile devices Lightweight, portable computing devices such as PDAs, smartphones, and handheld computers.

Modem port A port that connects to a standard telephone line, usually used to connect to the Internet or a local network, with a maximum speed of 56 kilobits per second (Kbps).

Monitor (or display screen) A common output device that displays text, graphics, and video.

Monitor port A port used to connect a monitor to a computer's graphic processing unit, located on the motherboard or video card.

Motherboard A large printed circuit board located in the system unit to which all other boards are connected; the motherboard contains the central processing unit (CPU), the memory (RAM) chips, and expansion card slots.

Mouse An input device used to enter commands and user responses into a computer.

Multicore A CPU that includes more than two microprocessors on a single integrated circuit. See also Dual-core.

Multifunction device (MFD) A device that has more than one purpose, often combining input and output capabilities.

Multimedia control key Usually found at the top of a keyboard, this type of key can be used to control or mute speaker volume.

Multimedia projectors Output devices used to display information on a screen for viewing by an audience.

Multitask The action of performing more than one task at the same time.

Network A group of two or more computers (or nodes) connected to share information and resources.

Network topology The layout and structure of a computer network.

Node Any object connected to a network—may be a computer or a peripheral device.

Nonimpact A type of printer that does not actually touch the paper.

Nonvolatile Permanent storage, as in read only memory (ROM); data remains even when power is shut down.

Notebook computer Also known as a laptop, this microcomputer is smaller than a desktop and designed to be portable.

Numeric keypad A bank of keys on a keyboard with which you can input numbers, it is located on the right side of a keyboard and is similar to an adding machine or calculator.

Open-source Software whose code is made available for developers to modify and use as they wish, usually available at no cost.

Operating system (OS) System software that controls the way in which a computer system functions, including the management of hardware, peripherals, and software; Microsoft Windows XP is an operating system.

Optical A type of storage process using a laser to read and write data; used by media such as CDs and DVDs.

OS See Operating system.

Output To retrieve data or information from a computer.

Output devices Computer hardware used to retrieve processed data and information from a computer; examples include the monitor, printer, and speakers.

P2P network See Peer-to-peer network.

PDA See Personal digital assistant.

Peer-to-peer (P2P) network A network in which each node can communicate directly with every other node, and which is often used for home and small business networks.

Peripheral A hardware device connected to a computer, but not located within the system unit, such as a monitor, printer, or mouse.

Permanent memory Memory used by storage devices to retain data and information.

Personal digital assistant (PDA) Also known as a hand-held computer, a small device that enables a user to carry digital information.

Personal firewall A software program or hardware device designed to prevent unauthorized access to a computer.

Phishing Email that masquerades as an authentic entity such as a bank or credit card company, requesting confidential information.

Pixel An abbreviated name for picture element.

Port An interface through which external devices are connected to the computer.

Presentation software A program used to create dynamic slideshows and generate speaker notes and audience handouts.

Printer An output device used to generate hard copy.

Process The term used to describe the action of a computer when it converts data into information.

Program A set of instructions used by a computer to perform certain tasks.

RAM See Random access memory.

Random Access Memory (RAM) A computer's temporary storage space or short-term memory and stored on chips located on the motherboard; measured in megabytes (MB) and gigabytes (GB). Known as volatile memory.

Read Only Memory (ROM) A set of memory chips located on the motherboard that stores data and instructions that cannot be changed or erased; it holds all the instructions the computer needs to start up. Also known as nonvolatile memory.

Refresh rate The speed at which the pixels are reilluminated, measured in cycles per second and expressed as hertz (Hz).

Resolution The measurement used to assess the clarity of an image on a monitor; determined by pixel density.

Restore point A record created by Windows XP for all of a computer's system settings.

Right-click The action of clicking the right mouse button.

Ring (or token-ring) topology A networking configuration in which all devices are set up in a circular layout; data flows in a circular fashion, in one direction only.

ROM See Read only memory.

S-video port A port used to connect ancillary video equipment, such as a television or projector to a computer.

Scanners Input devices used to convert hard copy documents or images into digital files.

Screen (or window) In a graphical user interface, the rectangular box that contains the program displayed on the monitor.

Scroll wheel A feature on some mouse pointing devices; rolling the wheel enables you to quickly move a page up or down within a window.

Sectors Wedge-shaped sections of a hard disk drive, each measured from the center point to the outer edge.

Serial port A type of port that sends data one bit at a time at speeds of up to 115 kilobits per second (Kbps). A mouse or modem may use a serial port to connect to a computer.

Server In a client/server network, the computer that manages shared network resources and provides access to the client computer when requested.

Smartphones Cell phones with additional computing capabilities or the ability to access the Internet.

Soft copy Data or information displayed on a monitor.

Software patches Quick software fixes provided to resolve an error found in program code until a software update can be issued.

Software updates Small, downloadable software modules that repair errors identified in commercial program code.

Spam Junk or unsolicited e-mail.

Speakers Output devices that allow the user to hear any auditory signals the computer sends.

Spreadsheet software A program with which you perform calculations and numerical analyses.

Spyware Software designed to capture personal and confidential information that resides on a computer and then send it elsewhere.

Star topology A flexible and frequently used network configuration for businesses, in which nodes connect to a central communication device known as a switch.

Storage To retain data or information for future use.

Stylus An input device used to write on a tablet computer or PDA.

Suite A collection of application software programs developed by the same manufacturer, bundled together and sold at a price that is usually less than the cost of purchasing each program individually.

Supercomputer A large, powerful computer typically devoted to specialized tasks. It is able to perform complex calculations quickly.

System software The set of programs that enables a computer's hardware devices and program software to work together; it includes the operating system and utility programs.

System unit The tower, box, or console that contains the critical hardware and electrical components of a computer.

Tablet computer A portable computer that features a screen that swivels and can be written on using advanced handwriting recognition software.

Toggle key A keyboard key that switches on or off each time it is pressed.

Token-ring topology See Ring topology.

Topology See Network topology.

Tracks Concentric circles on a hard disk drive.

Trojan horse A program that appears to be useful or desirable, but acts maliciously in the background after installation.

Universal serial bus (USB) port A versatile port used to connect a wide array of peripheral devices to a computer. USB 1.1 ports can send data at speeds of up to 12 megabits per second (Mbps). USB 2.0 ports can attain a rate of 480 Mbps.

User interface The features of a computer operating system that enable you to interact with the computer.

Utility program A component of system software, typically a small program used to perform routine maintenance and housekeeping tasks for the computer.

Virus Malicious code or program, usually installed on a computer without the user's knowledge or permission.

Volatile Temporary storage, as in random access memory (RAM); data is erased when power is shut down.

WAN See Wide area network.

Wide area network (WAN) A network composed of local area networks connected over long distances.

Window A box or screen that displays information or a program. Windows usually consist of title bars, toolbars, menu bars, and status bars. A window will always have a Minimize button.

Windows See Microsoft Windows.

Wireless network A network that connects using radio waves instead of wires or cable.

Word processing software A program used to create and edit written documents such as papers, letters, and resumes.

Worm A program that is able to replicate and spread from computer to computer without human interaction.

Zip drive A magnetic storage device used to save and retrieve data on Zip disks.

Zombie A computer that is controlled remotely and can be used to help spread viruses, spyware, and spam.

Index